The Lost Art of Being

The Lost Art of Being

Secrets to a Calm, Happy, Easy Life

Jacqui Macdonald

Matador
9 Priory Business Park,
Wistow Road, Kibworth Beauchamp,
Leicestershire. LE8 0RX
Tel: 0116 279 2299
Email: books@troubador.co.uk
Web: www.troubador.co.uk/matador
Twitter: @matadorbooks

ISBN 978 1789013 665
British Library Cataloguing in Publication Data.
A catalogue record for this book is available from the British Library.

Printed and bound in the UK by 4edge Limited
Typeset in Minion Pro 11pt by Troubador Publishing Ltd, Leicester, UK

Matador is an imprint of Troubador Publishing Ltd

I wrote this book for you.

ACKNOWLEDGEMENTS

Thank you to all my teachers, in particular Christine Arylo, Kristine Carlson, Eckhart Tolle, Marianne Williamson, Rupert Spira and my beloved Mooji. Thank you to my family, my babies, my fur babies, my PB and all my friends – you too have taught me more than you will ever know. Thank you to my beautiful students who have embraced and embodied the teachings to make powerful discoveries for themselves. Thank you to the trees for inspiring me every day and showing me how to be. And thank you to the Universe for… well, everything really.

CONTENTS

A BRIEF NOTE

Dearest Fabulous Reader,

I'm excited to be sharing this centuries-old wisdom about the art of being.

What you hold in your hands is a little book about slowing down, screwing the rules, following your heart and allowing the Universe to take care of your entire life. It is the long-lost secret to effortless happiness and tremendous inner peace.

I cannot claim to have written this book because, in truth, it wrote itself.

I was meant to go shopping that day.

As I was gathering my bag and purse, I became aware of words and phrases swirling impatiently within me, wanting to be written down. Thinking they would be nothing more than a few sentences, I pulled out my iPad and began typing on the Notes page.

Eight hours later, I was still there.

I then spent the entire weekend at my laptop… and the book came to life on the screen.

Over the following fortnight I dipped in and out – adding and editing whenever inspiration prompted.

And, whoops… I wrote a book.

Without.

Even.

Trying.

This book emerged from me without any effort, other than my time spent at the keyboard. There was no forward planning. No strategising. No agenda. No end goal in mind.

This is the perfect illustration of the lost art of being and will hopefully dispel any fears you might have that doing less results in under-achieving.

Quite the opposite.

Doing less enables you to become more.

I had been trying to write a book for over twenty years. I attended workshops and read books about how to write books. I followed all the advice and stuck to all the rules. And I worked really hard. But somehow it never quite happened.

But having learned over recent years how to slow down, do less, give up goals and listen to my heart… I simply allowed this book to be written.

This is the beauty of the art of being. It is a natural, effortless way to live and is the polar opposite to how convention dictates we should achieve our potential.

It is time to question convention.

AKA… screw the rules.

Because the rules are obscuring the truth.

The Universe flows through each of us in mystical, unfathomable, powerful ways – when we allow it.

The sacred secrets that you will find within the following pages will reveal everything the Universe wants you to know about how to give up the struggle and enjoy a calm, happy, easy life.

You will be encouraged to drop a belief system that prescribes hard work and effort. It will be exposed as nothing more than a set of thoughts that you have unwittingly bought in to. Fake rules that you are unconsciously following.

It is time to be liberated from such warped thinking and phony rules.

Because we all want an easy life, don't we?

Likewise, we all want happiness.

Granted, calm is not an aspiration for the young but as we mature we appreciate it, and long for it more and more.

Calm is your birth right.

As is happiness and ease.

Life should not be a struggle.

It's time to shatter the myth that the key to success is to do more.

What a topsy-turvy philosophy that is.

My hope is that this book will turn your world upside down and in doing so will return it to its rightful position.

The truth is simple: The less you do, the more you become.

That's because you allow the Universe to make it happen rather than trying to do everything yourself. After all, a Universe that keeps planets spinning and tides turning is surely more intelligent and powerful than we humans are?

And yet we cut ourselves off from that power.

What muppets we can be.

The reality is you don't have to struggle, drive or push to make your best life happen.

Isn't it a relief just to know that?

Your life is already programmed to be magnificent.

It's just that you can't see that right now because you're letting your human perspective over-rule your being. Your human is highly conditioned by society and is locked into belief systems and invisible rules that you never think to question, meaning you don't even know that you don't know.

You have become all human, no being - and this is the root of all your problems. The moment you realise this, you set yourself free and access your unlimited potential.

The being is the part of you that's full of the and magic and power.

You will soon come to experience this truth for yourself.

So relax.

Everything is about to change without you having to do a thing.

Other than to read this book, of course.

But that's all you have to do.

Just take the next step. Turn the next page.

No over-thinking, no planning, no rules or regimes. You do less, and yet you become so much more.

May your discovery of this truth be thrilling.

My being is tingling for your being.
See you on the other side.

Much love.
Jacqui

PRELUDE

HOW HUMAN BEINGS BECAME HUMAN DOINGS

Once upon a time, in its vast and infinite wisdom, the Universe decided to express itself through individual beings who could experience, for a limited time, a physical reality. It created many beings – tree beings, fish beings, dinosaur beings, ape beings - and over time they evolved and became more sophisticated until one day the human being arrived on the planet.

The human being was truly amazing. Its strength lay in its enormous capacity for thinking. Far beyond the capabilities of other beings, the human being was able to plan, strategize, imagine and create. It learned to make fire and it invented the wheel, and as centuries passed and new humans arrived in the physical realm, their brain-power enabled them to send rockets up to space and build computers that could rule the world.

This was a remarkable achievement and, to this day, human beings remain the most intelligent expression of the known Universe.

But they paid a sorry price for this superiority.

Somewhere along the line, human beings become so enthralled by their mental capabilities they lost sight of what was most important.

They forget they were beings.

In doing so they overlooked their greatest gift – their connection to a Universe that is naturally abundant and supportive, providing happiness no matter what.

Dazzled by their individual capacity for thinking and doing, they burned with ambition and took power into their own hands (and heads) to achieve their dreams. This was the moment they cut themselves off from the place within that was already encoded to enable them to reach their highest potential, effortlessly.

Instead they chose to strive.

The memory of themselves as an expression of the Universe was lost to all but a few, and so life for humans became highly fearful. Although their place at the top of the food chain was secure, they believed they were mere physical bodies and so avoiding mortality became their over-riding obsession.

These poor humans had forgotten they were beings, so rather than experiencing life from their inherent state of grace, they suffered.

As time passed, humans identified more and more with their mental prowess making it almost impossible for them to recall their divine origin. Even those who sensed the truth were so conditioned to solve all problems with their minds, they struggled to re-forge the universal connection - because the being cannot be thought back to reality. It is both before and beyond the brain.

Many humans spent lifetimes seeking with their minds, blinded by the great paradox that they were already everything that they were searching for.

Human beings became human doings – sophisticated and successful. Stressed and self-destructive.

It was malfunctioning on an epic scale.

Occasionally a human would experience a flicker of a memory of being. It was blissful and momentarily quenched all needs. But all too often it was fleeting and, as it faded, the human was left feeling vulnerable and alone again.

The saddest part of the story is that no human had to feel that way. If they had been less bound by their thinking and more attuned to their intuitive senses, they would have known with irrefutable clarity that human beings are never alone, nor are they ever in any danger.

To this day, despite their riches and success, humans continue to live an anxious and destructive existence.

In the mother of all ironies, their infatuation with staying alive has put the entire planet in critical danger.

But there is hope.

Today, all across Earth, humans are recalling the whole truth of who they are – divine spiritual beings having a physical experience. When this remembering occurs, all personal suffering is over and another sliver of global peace is restored.

The Universe continues to find ways of reaching out to those it believes are ready and willing to be reminded of their divine origin.

Its message is clear:

Life is not meant to be a struggle.

You have nothing to be afraid of.

Profound peace and happiness is your natural state as an extension of all that is.

Reclaim your power.

Regain your consciousness.

Reconnect with harmony.

Return to love.

This is the lost art of being.

PART ONE

WHAT IF YOU WERE TO SLOW EVERYT.H.I.N.G. D..O...W...N?

Slow down.
You're missing so much by going so fast.
Racing from one moment to the next.
Frantically searching for the magic ingredient that will make you happy.
So busy looking that you fail to see YOU ARE HAPPINESS ITSELF.
There is such irony in the human existence.
Slow down.
You're too busy.
Always on the go.
Slow down.
You do so much.
It's impossible to sustain.
Too much doing, not enough being.
Slow down.
Your entire experience of life changes when you slow it all down.
Eat slower.
Drink slower.
Walk slower.
Think slower.
Talk slower.
Are you even aware of the pace of which you do everything?
Could you become more conscious about slowing everything down?
Let's try it right now.

I invite you to read this book differently.
Slow down.
Allow the words time to touch your heart.
Slow down.
Touch.
Your.
Heart.
Slow down.

WHAT IF YOU COULD RECOGNISE THAT YOU ARE MAGICAL?

Pause for a moment and acknowledge that everything you have done in life so far has guided you to this exact moment.
How wonderful.
Slow down and notice the beauty.
The good, the bad and the ugly in your life was all part of your path to this precise second.
How magical.
You were destined to pick up this book. The Universe knows it's your time.
You are ready to remember the truth.
You are a human being, but you think you're merely human.
You've forgotten you are a being.
Big mistake.

Huge.

But very common.

Like millions of others, you're only living half a life.

You live as only human, oblivious to your true nature as a being.

This is the source of ALL your problems.

This book is designed to shake you up, wake you up and remind you of the WHOLE truth of who you are – a human being.

When you live as merely human, you leave out part of who you are.

That's why it feels like something is missing.

Something *is* missing.

A pretty significant something.

It's the very essence of who you are.

The Universe wants to remind you that you are a divine spirit, here in human form.

A human being.

Until you recognise and acknowledge both aspects of your existence – human AND being – you will feel like something is missing.

You will try to fill the void with a fabulous lifestyle, a sexy spouse, a great job and lots of money.

But even if you obtain all of that, you will still feel something is missing.

Only when you re-awaken to the reality of your true self will you feel whole, content and happy.

YOU HAVE CHOICE. CHOICE MEANS POWER.

What do you BELIEVE you need to feel whole, content and happy?
A loving partner?
Money?
Your dream home?
Your ideal job?
A beautiful body?
A cleaner diet?
Daily yoga?
Disciplined meditation?
A year in an Ashram?
All of the above?
Do you BELIEVE you need years of therapy or a library of self-help books to enable you weed out issues from your past and release negative energy and sadness?
Or… do you BELIEVE one little book could give you the greatest sense of happiness and peace that a human being can experience?
Notice you have a choice here.
You can CHOOSE what to BELIEVE.
So here you are, just a few pages in, and you've already come to crux of the truth about your reality.
WHATEVER YOU CHOOSE TO BELIEVE DEFINES YOUR EXPERIENCE OF LIFE.
It really is that simple.
Whether you choose to believe it or not is entirely up to you.

SO LET'S GET REALLY HONEST HERE...

What are you CHOOSING to BELIEVE?
Do you believe life must have certain conditions before you can feel happy?
Do you think you need better relationships, a bigger job, more money, more love?
Where did this thought come from?
Who said it?
Whose rules are you following?
What evidence is there that 'bigger, better, more' makes humans happy?
Is there not an ocean of evidence to refute this?
Flick through the pages of any celebrity magazine and you will see beyond doubt that even those who have everything – riches, fame, family and adulation – are not necessarily happy.
We see this, and yet we continue to believe collectively and individually that if we could just get the lottery win, the perfect body, the amazing lover the... (you fill in the blank) we would be happier.
These thoughts are so misaligned.
For the most part, your beliefs about what will make you happy are fundamentally flawed.
When you think you need possessions, circumstance or a situation to occur for you to be happy, you are buying into and perpetuating this myth.
But you can call time on this habit right now.
Notice that the thoughts you have about what will make you happy are simply thoughts.

And guess what… YOUR THOUGHTS ARE NOT REAL.
Thoughts are merely assumptions and impressions.
They are not facts.
They hold no weight.
If you continue to build your world around thoughts, it's like building your house on sand.
When sand shifts, as it inevitably does, all your foundations crumble.

QUESTION EVERYTHING

Your mind churns out millions of thoughts per day.
Thoughts are, by their very nature, assumptions and interpretations.
Concepts, ideas and judgements.
Notions.
Guesses.
Presumptions and projections.
You think you know how your day will pan out.
You predict what others are thinking.
You assume you know what you need to be happy.
But you don't.
You're guessing.
THOUGHTS ARE NOT FACTS.
And yet you believe them to be true and you build your world around them.
Here's the amazing thing…

You don't have to believe or buy into every thought you have.
Even the really convincing ones are just thoughts.
Thoughts are, by definition, illusory.
Stop believing in illusions.
Question everything.
Take nothing for granted.
Become aware that you can CHOOSE what you BELIEVE to be true.
You are the chooser.
Always.
When you don't see yourself as the chooser, you give away all your power.
You have more choice than you realise.
You have more power than you think.

SCREW THE RULES

Begin to notice that many of your thoughts arise from conditioning that has no real substance. Much of what you believe appears to be true only because it's what everyone else believes.
We have become enslaved by invisible rules that nobody thinks to question.
This represents a great challenge for humanity
We have become sheep.
We think we're really clever, but we are sheep.

Baaaaaaaa.

We believe things just because it's what everyone else believes.

Once upon a time most humans thought the world was flat.

Everyone believed it.

Did that make it true?

Nowadays, most humans believe that life is a struggle and that happiness is hard to come by.

Does that make it true?

Is it true for you?

Most humans believe that they are a physical body governed by the mind.

Is that what you believe?

Or could it be that there is more to being human than the physical body and mind?

Is there any possibility that there could be another perspective to being human that you are missing out on because you are conditioned to think like everyone else?

Question everything.

Take back your power.

Start seeing life through your own eyes and wake up to the truth.

It's your time to wake up to the truth.

Continuing to read this book signifies that you are CHOOSING to BELIEVE that the rules are fake, and that happiness is not as elusive or complicated as you had previously believed it to be.

You have acknowledged that there may be more to the human existence than just a body and a mind, and that

somewhere beyond the physical lies the answers to a calm, happy, easy life.
This is a watershed moment.
A line in the sand.
You've admitted it now.
There's no going back.
From this moment on, what's true for you is that profound happiness is attainable, potentially in the blink of an eye.
Blink.
A new moment.
A fresh start.
A new beginning.
Another chance to choose happiness.
Grab it.

THE SIMPLE TRUTH ABOUT YOUR MIND

This is not complicated.
The only thing complicated is your mind.
Your mind is a highly sophisticated machine because its primary function is to keep your body alive.
Have you ever thought about that?
The brain is simply another organ in the body, alongside the liver, stomach, lungs and heart, that has a job to do.
The job of the organs is to keep your body alive.
The lungs take in breath.
The heart pumps blood and oxygen around the body.

The stomach digests food creating fuel and energy.
The liver keeps the system clean and functioning.
Each of these organs has an important job to do in keeping your body alive.
That is the primary function of your organs.
Your survival.
Not your happiness.
The same is true of your brain.
It is just another organ tasked with keeping your body alive.
Do you ever get annoyed with your mind?
Why does my brain produce thoughts that make me feel like shit?
My mind is driving me crazy!
Why won't the voice in my head just SHUT UP!?
Does this sound familiar?
Your frustrations are misguided.
Getting annoyed with your brain for not producing happier thoughts is like getting annoyed with your cat because it won't bark.
It's not the cat's job to bark.
In fact, cats can't bark.
It's not your mind's job to make you happy.
Your mind can't make you happy.
This is a critical understanding.
Stop expecting the cat to bark.
Cats can't bark.
The mind can't make you happy.

YOU ARE PROGRAMMED TO BE PARANOID

The primary job of the mind is, like all the other organs, to keep your body alive.
To do this it runs two major programmes.
Programme number one is Paranoia.
It is the job of the mind to be on the lookout at all times for situations, people or circumstances that may be a threat to your existence.
It's like having the most OCD bodyguard in charge of your personal security 24/7. It will it warn you not to walk down dark alleys at night, and just to make sure you're really paying attention it will flood your imagination with a movie-reel of images of what MIGHT happen to you should you walk down that alley.
Chances are you'll pay attention and find a different route.
The mind is really good at its job.
Its job is to keep your body alive.
You mind will also alert you if you're at risk of putting yourself in a situation where you could look like a fool.
Looking like a fool could jeopardise your valuable standing amongst your peer group.
As far as the mind is concerned, looking like you've got your act together and projecting a winning image to the outside world is essential.
Weakness could result in ostracism from the pack.
When you're ostracised, you're vulnerable.
You could be picked off.
Pulled down.
Game over.

The mind does not want you to be vulnerable.
Its job is to keep you alive.
In your mind's eye, your reputation and your survival are intrinsically linked.
You MUST show family, friends and Facebook followers that you are well and truly in the game.
This is what the mind tells you.
Whether you CHOOSE to BELIEVE it is entirely up to you.

YOU ARE DRIVEN BY DESIRE

The second powerful programme that the mind runs is Desire.
Actually, Desire is a sub-programme of Paranoia.
The two go hand-in-hand.
Paranoia fuels desire.
The paranoia that you might a) die or b) be ostracised (thereby putting yourself at risk of death) automates a powerful drive and desire within you to want bigger, better, more so that you feel safe.
You want a bigger house, a better car, the perfect partner, a baby, more money, more fame, more followers on Instagram… ultimately because you want to feel accepted and safe within the pack.
Can you recognise this?
Desire arises from sub-conscious paranoia.

The marketing industry understands this and uses it to sell you stuff.
Buy this amazing handbag, take a selfie and put it in Facebook.
Everyone will think you've gone up in the world.
Another step up in the imagined hierarchy of the pack.
You NEED this handbag.
Your mind agrees, and it embellishes the story…
You also need a fancy job title, a swanky lifestyle, more money.
Show the world how great you are.
Then your position in the pack will be safe.
When you CHOOSE to BELIEVE your mind (which is only doing its job to keep your body alive), you swallow this ridiculous story.
Hook, line and sinker.
But you have a choice. You always have a choice.
You have more power than you realise.

YOUR LONGINGS ARE ENTIRELY MISGUIDED

The mind has another secret weapon up its sleeve.
It knows that you have a sense that something is missing.
That's because something *is* missing.
You've lost touch with your being.
You don't feel complete, so you search for stuff that will make you feel better.

You want a baby, a purposeful job, an amazing relationship, the perfect home.
You want these things because you don't feel whole, but you don't know why you don't feel whole.
You think something out there will make you feel whole.
It won't.
Nothing out there can fill the void, but you don't see it.
Your longings are misguided.
You want stuff because you want to be accepted by the pack.
You want stuff because you feel like something is missing.
Your desire for stuff is overwhelming.
Your quest for attaining becomes a lifetime mission.
This distracts you from your real mission.
Your real mission is to remember the truth of who you are – a human being.
But the mind is powerful and its programming for desire dominates your existence.
When you stop wanting things to be different from the way they are, you give yourself space.
With space comes the gift of clarity.
Clarity brings you one step closer to your being.

NO WONDER YOU FEEL SO AFRAID

You will soon begin to see the truth.
The role of the mind – the organ that governs your entire physical experience – is not to make you happy.

The role of the mind is to keep your body alive.
Its job is to keep you locked in a very human experience, believing you are mortal.
The mind does not want you to have any concept of your immortality.
It doesn't want you to take any risks.
This is how the human is programmed.
It's very smart – excellent software for keeping you and the entire species alive.
But the programme has been corrupted.
Humans have become so obsessed with their personal survival they don't even care if they take down the whole planet.
Unbelievable irony.
This is a problem on a global scale, but also for you personally.
You don't feel safe.
Paranoia has gone berserk.
Desire is running riot.
You feel out of control, because you are.
You are malfunctioning.
You know this.
It feels terrifying.
But it isn't necessarily terminal.
There is a way to restore yourself to factory settings.
All you need to do is turn yourself off and back on again.
Are you ready for your reboot?

YOU HAVE NOTHING TO BE AFRAID OF

As a human being, you were created in perfect balance.
You were given a mind and body to experience and enjoy a short-term physical reality with its highs and lows.
You were also given a soul and that was like having the entire Universe at your fingertips, so you could always feel connected to the infinite power that keeps the planets spinning and the tides turning.
Yes; that very same power pulses within you.
The same power that enables an acorn to become a mighty oak.
How else did you grow from an embryo into an adult?
It's the very same universal power and it resides in the heart of your being.
The balance between the human and the being is glorious.
The physical, time-bound body imbued with the grace of the timeless.
Your challenge was to maintain that balance by enjoying your human experience while remembering the truth of your being.
But you blew it.
Well… not just you.
Millions of us blew it.
We got carried away with the human and lost sight of the being.
And suddenly the party isn't so great anymore. We've drunk too much and the music's gone all drum & bass.
We want to go home.
But we can't remember where home is.

THERE'S A MAP INSIDE YOUR HEART

Home is the infinity of the Universe.
The good news is you can't ever actually lose your way home because it's who you are.
It's just that you've forgotten that.
You're like a wave trying to find its way back to the ocean.
Silly, isn't it?
If you rely on your mind to guide you home, you will continue to be lost.
You will go around in circles, driving yourself ever more crazy.
You cannot think your way home.
You won't find the roadmap inside your head.
If you want to get back to the truth of who you are, you must stop relying on your mind. It was the one who got you in this mess in the first place, remember?
The answer is to get out of your head and into your heart.
The roadmap is in your heart.

THE MAP

Slow down as you read this part.
Less head, more heart.
Less thinking, more feeling.
Less stress, more grace.

Less strategising, more allowing.
Less doing, more being.
Less grasping, more attracting.
Less holding on, more letting go.
Less judgement, more acceptance.
Less blame, more forgiveness.
Less attachment, more freedom.
Less hate, more compassion.
Less mind, more soul.
Less fear, more love.
Less suffering, more peace.
Less human, more being.
Less head, more heart.
Read this page again.
Even more slowly.
It is the roadmap to guide you home.

RESISTANCE

I can't let my heart rule my head.
Everyone knows that's a recipe for disaster.
Financial ruin.
Social suicide.
See how the mind is REALLY good at its job?
See how it runs a programme of fear-based thinking to keep you in its thrall?

Any whiff that you might be considering over-ruling its authority and it will up the ante, generating thoughts that are even more fearful and doom-ridden than before.
It will produce all manner of notions to dissuade you from this folly of listening to your heart.
The mind is very good at its job.
It is brilliant at keeping your body alive.
If your mind is throwing up resistance, notice that you can CHOOSE whether to BELIEVE it.
Thoughts are not facts.
Even if they feel very real, they are not facts.
If you can manage to over-ride the mind, even for a few precious moments, you may notice that somewhere within you there is a nagging suspicion that you're discovering something important here.
So let's keep going.
The mind is not who you are.
It is an organ with a job to do.
When you BELIEVE every thought the mind produces, you will probably stay alive but it may not be a particularly joyous existence.
The job of the mind is not to make you happy.
If you want to be happy, follow your heart.

DISCOVERING YOUR TRUE HEART

Errrrr… isn't my heart just another organ designed to keep me alive?

Yes.

When you're referring to the physical heart, this is true.

It's just a pump.

An important pump.

But a pump nonetheless.

However, there is another heart within you that is recognised and honoured in Eastern traditions, but you don't give it so much respect if you were raised with Western conditioning.

This is your great existential challenge.

You think your physical heart, the pump, is the only one you have.

You've been far too busy doing seemingly important things in your fast-paced, hi-tech life to pause and check in with your true heart – the heart of who you are.

The what?

Exactly.

You don't even remember that who you are (not what you are) also has a heart.

Your human body has a heart – the pump.

Your being also has a heart.

Does something inside you remember that?

DISCOVERING YOUR TRUE HAPPINESS

You are a human being.
A being who happens to be here in human form.
But first and foremost, a being.
Your human form is the dynamic aspect of your existence that gets up, goes to work, eats lunch, goes shopping, has sex, sleeps, and complains about life… a lot.
Your human form is governed by your mind.
It lives a very physical existence and believes itself to be mortal.
It is obsessed with staying alive.
It has become so focused on your physical survival that it forgot the truth of who you are.
It's forgotten you're a human being, and that the being aspect of your existence is immortal.
Your being is connected to all that is.
It wants for nothing.
It enjoys a very pleasant existence.
It is naturally happy.
You say all you want is to be happy.
And yet you overlook the fact that there is an aspect of you that is the source of all happiness.
Wouldn't you like to be a little more being and a little less human?
You are already both.
But you choose not to believe this.
You choose to believe the thoughts that say you are merely human.
Take back your power.

Question these thoughts.
Screw the rules.
Enable the tiny shift in perception required to recall the lost art of being, and in doing so reinstate your natural peace and happiness.

DISCOVERING YOUR SOUL

Your being is who you are without the constructed story of the human.
It's you; pure you.
Stripped back.
Acoustic.
Just you.
Your human is busy. Busy climbing the hierarchy. Busy staying safe. It has a lot of things to do.
Your being, however, has nothing to do. No goals to reach, no stuff to buy, nothing to say, nowhere to go.
It is simply being.
This is the very heart of who you are.
You might call it your soul, your spirit, your divine essence or your inner self.
Labels don't matter.
The only thing important is that you recognise there's a really cool part of yourself that simply exists.
You don't even have to know or believe that this part of

you is an extension of the entire Universe and therefore has you plugged into infinite power, peace and happiness.
That knowledge will come.
First you have to acknowledge the truth.
You are a human being.
Not merely a human.
A human being.

EVERY MOMENT IS ANOTHER CHANCE TO CHOOSE

Einstein famously said: "The greatest existential decision you will ever make is whether you live in a hostile universe or a friendly universe."
That dude knew.
He was one of the beings who tried to point us back to the truth of who we are.
Einstein, one of world's greatest scientists, was giving clues to how the Universe really works.
When you choose to identify as a human, the Universe will seem hostile because the human experience is governed by the mind which is programmed to run paranoid, fear-based thinking.
When you choose to identify as a being, the Universe will seem friendly because the being is governed by love.
Whatever decision you make will define your entire

experience of life.
Head or heart?
Human or being?
Hostile or friendly?
Or a little bit of both?
Whatever you CHOOSE to BELIEVE will define your reality.
Choose wisely.

RECOGNISING YOUR BEING. IT'S KIND OF IMPORTANT

Your being is pure consciousness, out of which your entire human existence is experienced.
Without consciousness, you could not be human.
Without your being, you could not be you.
And yet you persist in ignoring your being and giving all your attention to your human.
Your human has a life which seems exciting and dramatic.
But without your being, it would be nothing.
Your being is the 'I am' principle that is there before all else.
There cannot be knowledge of anything in the Universe if there is not first a sense of 'I am'.
'I am' is the definitive of the human being.
The concept of 'I am' must be present before any other sensation or experience can be perceived.

I am hot.
I am hungry.
I am happy.
I am your friend.
I am here.
None of these states or emotions are possible without the preceding principle of the foundational state of 'I am'.
So the being is kind of important
The being does not get drawn into the drama of your life.
The being just is.
It is the allowing entity out of which arises the essential sense of 'I am'.
Without it, your life would cease to exist.
No being.
No human.
Why do you give your being such little attention?

HANGING OUT WITH YOUR BEING

Fortunately, the being does not crave attention like the human does.
The being just is.
It already has everything it could possible want because it exists as part of the energetic forcefield known as the Universe.
Your being is slice of the universal cake.

You are a slice of the universal cake.
The entire Universe can be tasted within that slice.
When you recognise this magical truth, life begins to get easier.
You start giving more attention to the being.
This means less focus on the human.
When the human has less focus, the stress, troubles and suffering of the person also fade respectively.
Does that make sense?
Life for the human is tough.
Life for the being is effortless.
If you want a calm, happy easy life, start hanging out with your being.
Say hi to your being.
Get to know it.
Feel its presence.
Acknowledge it.
Enjoy it.
Honour it.
Love it.
Allow it to emerge within you, in doing so removing much of the importance of the human drama and stress.
Spend time with it.
Spend time as it.
You are it.
You can never not be it.
Notice this.
Feel it.
Enjoy it.
Give it centre stage in your life and relegate the human to the chorus line where it can high-kick to its heart's content.

The drama of the human will recede into the wings, taking with it the stress of the person. Your life will become infused with a spotlight of pure consciousness as your being becomes the rightful star of the show.

THE BEAUTY OF BEING

Your being has none of the hang-ups of the human.
It just is.
Your being does not judge.
Nor does it jostle for position within the pack.
The being is neutral.
It observes, as pure consciousness.
It just is.
It experiences life moment by moment.
It does not carry the hangovers of yesterday, nor does it anticipate the pains of tomorrow.
It just is.
Your being sees everything.
It is the foundational principle of your very existence.
It is the flowerbed of your life, out of which both blossoms and weeds will emerge.
It stays neutral, knowing its place as the allowing principle.
It witnesses everything.
It reacts to nothing.
It just is.

The being cannot be defined, labelled or boxed-in like the human can.
Acknowledge this within you, and witness your whole life open to the infinite.

DITCHING THE PETTINESS OF THE HUMAN

The human lives in the past and the future.
It hangs on to old memories and uses them as evidence that life is hostile.
It constantly worries about the future.
This programmes the future to be just like the past.
The human is judgemental.
It is always trying to figure out where it stands in the pack so is constantly assessing whether it is better/smarter/slimmer/richer/prettier than the human it is talking to.
Notice this.
It's not very nice.
The human is highly defensive.
The human experience is governed by the mind and the mind is programmed to be paranoid.
For the same reason, the human must always be right.
This is extremely dull.
The human wants to be in control all the time because life as a human is fearful and it will grasp onto any shred of influence it can to feel a tiny bit safer.
The control-freakery is also dull.

The being is free from such pettiness.
The being lives in the moment.
It knows that this moment is all there really is.

THE MOST IMPORTANT DISCOVERY OF MY LIFE

Oh. My. God.
I never imagined life could feel this blissful.
Because the mind's best imagining can't dream of such euphoria.
I never understood the truth of my existence.
Because the mind's greatest understanding can't compute such purity.
I never realised that life could be so easy.
Because the mind's best reckonings can't fathom such grace.
It is beyond the realm of thinking.
I see that now.
I had been giving so much power to my mind.
What a fool!
The mind is limited.
It wears blinkers.
It blinds the truth.
Or at least it tries.
Remove the blinkers and you reveal the truth.

Beyond your mind an entire Universe awaits.
And it is beautiful, blissful and effortless beyond belief…

FINDING MY TRUE POWER

I lived 40 years as merely human.
Then suddenly… an awakening.
When I realised I was a human being, my life exploded with effortless grace.
Pain from the past was recognised as merely a memory that my mind was hanging on to.
Worries about the future disappeared back into the fantasy-world from which they had emerged.
I realised my entire identity was a story that my mind was perpetuating.
When I dropped my story, I felt liberated.
Rather than think about how life ought to be, based on my previous experiences and future expectations, I began to just live it, moment by moment.
No more planning, strategising or trying to take the bull by the horns.
And you won't believe what happened…
Rather than the bull rampaging around my life wrecking everything in its path, it lay down at my feet and invited me to climb on board.

When I stopped trying to control everything, I finally began to ride the power.

LIFE DOESN'T HAVE TO BE HARD

I am not claiming to live every moment of my life in perfect serenity.
I am a human being.
As a human I experience moments of stress, discomfort, anxiety and sadness.
Moments.
They never stay for long.
How times have changed.
Previously, I lived my entire life in varying degrees of pissed-offness.
I drunk a lot of wine to dull the pain.
There were moments of happiness.
Moments. They never stayed for long.
For the most part, there was suffering.
Life wasn't much fun back then
But these days it's different.
I am a human being.
As a being I am tapped into the infinite wellspring of love and happiness and that is my natural essence. That might sound airy and even kind of cliché but you know what? It feels bloody amazing.

And life is so easy.
Why do we make it so hard?
It really doesn't have to be so hard.
You are a human being who gives far too much attention and energy to your humanness and nowhere near enough to your beingness.
It is the root source of all stress in your life.
The moment you begin to shift your perspective to elevate the importance of your being, the human stuff fades and life becomes sweeter and sweeter.
The beauty is you can begin right now.
Be mindful of your thoughts.
Notice when you're getting sucked back into fear-based thinking.
Take back control and reach for your most loving thought.
It doesn't have to be pure love. Any glint of compassion is an upgrade on where you were before. And so the journey begins.
Your being will guide you, if you let it.
Slow down. Listen. Just be.

WOW...WOW...WOW...

Realising that I am first and foremost a being has been the most exhilarating discovery of my life.
I'm not merely human, I'm a being too.

I'm not merely a being, I'm human too.
Recognising the whole truth of my existence has left me wanting for nothing.
Oh trust me… The human can still be a diva.
She likes nice holidays and money in the bank.
But the being sees her quirks and remains blissfully neutral.
The human can get stroppy if things aren't going her way.
The being remains unruffled.
The human is not immune to bad weather, irritating admin and the challenge of raising teenagers.
In these moments I CHOOSE to identify with the being.
This is the truth of who I am.
A human being.
Perfectly imperfect.
There is such peace in this acceptance of my truth.

YOU ARE A HUMAN BEING

There are many kinds of beings.
Spiritual beings, tree beings, animal beings.
You are a human being.
This means you are human version of a being.
Human beings can see, hear, smell, touch, taste, and think.
Boy, can they think.
The human being is highly sophisticated.

But it is ultimately a being.
The brain wants you to believe that you are only human – a body and mind, of which it is the boss.
The brain exists in the physical world and cannot get its head around anything non-physical.
The brain cannot compute the non-physical.
The brain only recognises the human.
But you are more than human.
You are a human being.
You know what it means to be a human.
You are living that experience right now.
But what does it mean to be a being?

BEING IS THE ESSENCE OF THE UNIVERSE

Everything that exists with sentience in the Universe is a being of some description.
In other words, everything that breathes is a being.
There are fish beings, bird beings, animal beings and human beings.
Some might argue that they are also plant and tree beings. Even rock beings.
And while it's true that everything in existence is ultimately an expression of the Universe, it is simpler to focus on what we know to have 'life' within it.
I.e. living creatures such as birds, fish, animals and humans.

So, what is it that gives these creatures life?
What enables them to breathe?
What facilitates the functioning of the senses?
It is the beingness.
Nothing more.
Nothing less.
It is the divine essence of the Universe that is simply there, expressed in fish form, bird form, animal form or in your case – human form.
Each form comes with its own physical strengths and weaknesses.
In the case of humans, we have evolved to contain the most sophisticated brain in the universal kingdom, enabling us to be top of the food chain.
This is great news for our survival.
But bad news for our happiness.

QUESTION CONDITIONING

Human beings have evolved with such awesome brains that we can launch rockets into space.
But we have become so obsessed with using these brains and pushing them to their limits that we have lost track of the fact that we are, in essence, beings.
Everything we value in this physical world comes from brain power.
We give all credit to the human.

A remarkable species.
Remarkably successful.
Remarkably destructive.
Remarkably unhappy.
Most humans rely entirely on the brain.
It has convinced us that it has all the answers.
It has convinced you that it has all the answers.
It has been so convincing that it has over-shadowed your memory of yourself as a being.
This over-shadowing has been a long time in the making.
Thousands and thousands of years.
As evolution occurred and human beings climbed the food chain, something magical was left behind.
Our ancestors confirmed and re-confirmed that mental prowess was the key to life.
We inherited these beliefs, this conditioning.
And we continue to perpetuate them today.

QUESTION EVERYTHING

It's rare to find a human being who stops for a minute in this hectic world and thinks… *wait a minute, who exactly am I?*
But these beings do exist.
They exist in temples in Thailand, in caves in India and sometimes in suburban streets in England.

You'd be surprised.
When this critical question is asked, all heaven breaks loose.
A sudden and dramatic memory is reignited and within a flash these beings re-cognise exactly who they are.
I am a being.
I am a human being.
And life is never the same again.
No longer are we beings held by the belief systems that keep others stuck on the wheel of suffering.
We remember the truth of who we are.
Human beings.
Divine beings that just so happen to be expressing in human form right now.
Ultimately, beings that are the very essence of the Universe itself.
That is what we are.
That is who you are.
Kinda cool, huh?

NOT ONLY HUMAN AFTER ALL

As a human I have a physical body and a physical heart.
As a being I have a non-physical presence and a non-physical heart.
It's the non-physical heart that you can tap into to experience your natural bliss.

Your brain is probably already trying to locate this non-physical heart?
That's because it believes that only the physical is real.
This is a deeply flawed philosophy.
There is so much more to reality than the physical.
The human is highly cynical.
The mind does not want to lose its authority.
It has a job to do.
Its job is to keep your body alive.
Even now it is generating thoughts that will encourage you to question what you're reading.
It will keep on generating these thoughts until one of them sticks.
And you will put down this book and think... *phew – that was a near miss, I nearly got pulled into a load of spiritual crap there.*
And off you will go making money, doing jobs, eating, sleeping, surviving.
But you will not be truly, madly, deeply happy.
You will always feel like something is missing.

HUMAN AND BEING IN BALANCE

As a human I have physical needs.
I need to eat, sleep, drink water and look after my body.
As a human I have a life that I must tend to.

I have children and pets to look after.
I have a home to pay for and keep clean.
I have family, friends and a job.
A fairly typical human life.
As a being, an expression of the entire Universe, I can observe my human experiencing life.
I do not give all my attention to the human and its mind which is full of stories to distract me and keep me scared.
I take little notice of my mind. I am a being, enjoying a human experience.
As are you.
Life as a human being is beautiful. It allows me to be present with the stuff that really matters. I have tremendous powers of discernment meaning I can sniff out BS from a mile away. The human is sometimes tempted to get involved with the drama.
The being says… 'Let it be'.
The being knows that life is playing out and revealing itself with unfathomable perfection.
The human thinks it can do better.
Ha!
Such arrogance I have as a human.
But as a being I can experience the wholeness of myself entirely without assumption or expectation.
It is just as it is.
Such lightness. Such wonder. Such a buzz!
This is the truth of my happiness.

HUMAN LIFE CAN BE HELL

Occasionally a story will snag me.
When something shitty happens I get pulled from my neutrality and immersed into the full-on drama of the human.
That's when the trouble starts.
Human life is stressful.
Bills to pay. Children to raise. Relationships to tend to. Work to be done.
Not to mention the threats to humanity – global warming, international terrorism and insane world leaders.
When I only inhabit this world and forget about the truth of who I am, life is scary as hell.
In these moments, I have given my life to my mind.
I have handed all my power to one who cannot be trusted.
I am believing every thought that the mind is producing.
Thoughts that are assumptions, guesses and speculation about what the future might hold.
Thoughts that are not real.
I am investing all my emotion and energy into an existence that is not real.
I am building my house on sand.
And so I catch myself, and I return my attention to the truth.
I am a human being.
First and foremost a being.
A divine expression of the Universe, naturally tuned into an infinite source of serenity and love.
This can never not be who I am.
All else is imagined.
Once more, I am at peace.

HELL IS NOT REAL

This is not about being in denial.
I don't go running off to some fantasy bubble every time life gets tough.
Quite the opposite.
When I believe the mind – I'm in the fantasy.
When I open my eyes – I remember the truth.
I am not in denial.
Not anymore.
I was in denial for the forty years that I failed to recognise the truth of myself.
I believed what my mind told me:
You need to work hard.
You need lots of money.
You need to be in a relationship.
You need to have a baby.
You need to be someone. SOMEONE!
What a load of crap.
I built my world around these beliefs – expecting them to make me happy.
How foolish.
But then I remembered my truth.

THE ONLY HELL IS IN YOUR MIND

Profound, lasting, immeasurable happiness arises when you acknowledge your being.
Happiness cannot come from the mind.
It is not the job of the mind to instil a deep and irrefutable sense of tranquillity and joy within you.
It is the job of the mind to keep your body alive.
It is the job of the mind to instil a sense of fear and potential doom within you.
When you live as only human, you are enslaved to the programming of the mind.
This programming consists of paranoia and endless desire.
No matter what you do, you will always feel vulnerable.
No matter what you have you will always want more.
The Universe will always seem hostile.
This is how the mind works.
This is its job.
It is very good at its job.

RECOGNISING RESISTANCE

The mind is hugely powerful and will generate whatever thoughts it can to prevent you from making the greatest discovery in the human kingdom.

It will tell you that these kinds of existential enquiries will make you sadder, not happier.
The more you persist in exploring your non-physical heart, the more resistance your mind will create.
Be warned.
It may make you feel so low, so angry and depressed that you will wish you never started down this road.
It will throw everything at you to stop this line of enquiry.
It's just doing its job.
So beware.
But be gentle.
Don't be angry with the mind.
It is only doing its job.
It knows no better.

IGNORING THE PESKY MIND

The human in you is anxious right now
The being in you is ecstatic.
Keep going.
Keep reading.
Don't give up.
Don't give this to your mind.
Allow your attention to ebb into your non-physical heart.
It may be located around or close to the physical heart.
It is sometimes called the heart-centre and you might be

able to sense it around the middle of your chest.
Or not.
You may feel it elsewhere.
Perhaps not even within your body.
Don't try to find it with your mind.
Your mind will send you down a cul-de-sac.
It's not so much a case of locating it physically.
Sense it. Feel it. Tune in.
Allow it to emerge within you.
Like a flower opening to the morning sun.

CHOOSING WHAT TO BELIEVE

Shitty things happen in life.
We lose things. We lose our phones. We lose jewellery. We lose our jobs. We lose all our money. We lose our houses.
We lose lovers. We lose loved ones. Forever.
These shitty things make the mind leap into action.
Its job is to keep us alive.
It believes that losing things makes us vulnerable.
It will produce scary thoughts again and again.
When we lose all our money we feel very vulnerable.
The mind tells us we have to do whatever it takes to get the money back.
The only option is a struggle and a battle that we must undertake for our survival.

Whatever it takes.
Money and survival are more important than happiness, right?
This is a thought produced by the mind.
Just because the mind (whose job it is to keep us alive) produces a thought, doesn't mean you have to believe it.
It is up to you to CHOOSE what you want to BELIEVE.
Oh and by the way… this is not a choice between happiness and survival – which is what the mind might be telling you right now (crafty bugger.)
You can have both.
Remember you're a human being.
There are two aspects to your existence.
You are a divine spirit having a physical experience.
Go to the mind to keep your body alive.
But don't go there for your happiness.
Go to the heart for your happiness. Your non-physical heart. The heart of your being.
Live in total harmony with your physical body and your spiritual being.
Be happy and stay alive.
Live in balance – honouring your human and your being.
This is the sacred secret to happiness and inner peace.

YOUR BODY IS BOSSED BY YOUR MIND

Thoughts can be so powerful that you believe them into existence and they create a physical reaction in the body.
That's because the body and mind are all part of being human. They work together to keep the human alive. They are on the same team.
Team human.
You lose all your money and the mind says: "That's it, you're ruined, you're going to end up sleeping on the streets, you will become a junkie and you will die."
If you CHOOSE to believe these thoughts, it will hurt.
Your body will go into panic mode; tightness in the tummy, the chest and shoulders, sweaty palms, shallow breathing, unusual toilet activity, the works.
Your entire physical body will believe and be living out the belief that the onset of death is possible.
This is a highly unpleasant feeling, designed to spur you into action and do whatever it takes to get your money back, so this horrendous physical feeling will go away.
You see – the mind is an expert at survival.
It will save your physical life.
But it won't give you that profound feeling of bliss, peace and universal abundance that is the natural fragrance of the heart.

YOUR BEING IS BOSSED BY NOBODY

But how can I be happy if I'm living on the streets injecting heroin?

Hang on… let's rewind.

That scenario will only become reality if you CHOOSE to BELIEVE that it's true.

But guess what.

You do have another option.

You could thank the body and mind for sending you thoughts of doom and the accompanying physical symptoms.

And then you could CHOOSE not to BELIEVE those thoughts. Which are, after all, only thoughts.

You can always CHOOSE to remember that you are a human being and while the human part of you may be having a tough time in this physical world, the being part of you – which is actually more real than the human – is perfectly happy, peaceful and content.

The being doesn't NEED anything.

The being already has everything.

The being is one facet of the diamond that is the entire Universe.

All that exists is reflected within it.

It wants for nothing.

When you CHOOSE to experience your existence from this perspective, all your woes dissolve.

What is not physical cannot be physically threatened.

You are a being. Know this and witness the fears, worries and problems of the physical world simply melt away.

YOU REALLY DON'T HAVE TO STRUGGLE

But I feel very human and I have no money and my lover dumped me and IT HURTS LIKE HELL!

Of course it does.

This is all very real for you.

You have been conditioned (by your mind, and your ancestor's minds) that you need money, a lover, a family, a home, a car and several holidays per year in order to be happy.

You don't need any of these things to be happy.

You are happiness itself.

You are already a being that is abundant with joy and grace. But you are so transfixed by your physical 'reality' that you cannot see what is true.

When you stop giving your entire life to your mind, you will fall into step with your true self and begin experiencing such spontaneity and synchronicity in your life that it will feel like heaven on earth.

This is the divine law of the Universe.

Get back in touch with your natural state and the entire Universe will conspire to re-affirm your happiness. Life will unfold with unspeakable beauty and you will not have to struggle for anything.

But you must make that leap of faith.

You must be brave enough to fire the mind as CEO of you and give the role to the heart.

Yikes.

THE SPECTACULAR POWER OF DOING LESS

Do you believe that the answer to any and all of your problems is to do less, not more?

Our conditioning as a species is so strong that the concept of doing less is almost scandalous.

Nowhere in our society are we encouraged to solve problems by doing not much at all.

That's because collectively we've lost faith.

We've lost belief in a Universe that always has our best interests at heart and is already programmed to ensure each of us reaches our maximum potential for happiness.

Instead, we take it upon ourselves to think up solutions and act assertively to overcome challenges and be the best we can be.

Sometimes it works out fine. We fix the issue, and move on.

But rather like the story of the boy who used his fingers to plug holes in the dyke to hold back the flood, the leaks just keep on coming and eventually we run out of fingers.

Our existence becomes dedicated to looking out for the biggest leaks and plugging them as best we can.

How exhausting!

We fear doing nothing because, to continue the metaphor, we are terrified of being engulfed by the flood.

We think we know what's best for us, and it does not involve being overwhelmed by a torrent of water.

But how do we know that for sure?
Maybe the flood will bring untold riches?
Perhaps it will wash us to new pastures with fresh opportunities and the chance to experience happiness far beyond our current comprehension?
We rarely find out because we take it upon ourselves to hold back the water.
In doing so, we hold back the natural flow of life by thinking we know what's best.
The beauty of doing less and letting life flow naturally is that solutions and outcomes effortlessly occur, and rather than having to bust a gut figuring things out for ourselves, the answer is spontaneously presented.
We then simply take the next step.
This makes life a lot less stressful.
It's the difference between doing life and being life.
But it takes balls to turn your back on centuries of conditioning, not to mention pressure from your family and friends who will be expecting you to act like everyone else.
Trust me, you'll get a lot of grief when you choose to embrace the philosophy of less doing, more being.
But ultimately you won't care because you've shattered the myth about fitting in and discarded the need for approval.
You'll be so chilled out and happy that you won't give a fig about what others think.
And somewhere along the line you'll meet another human being who is so inspired by your liberated outlook on life that they'll also make the shift.
And a little more peace is restored.

THE BLISS OF GOING WITH THE FLOW

Isn't doing less irresponsible?
No, burying your head in the sand is irresponsible.
Pretending that the problem isn't there is irresponsible.
Seeing it, acknowledging it, accepting it and going with the flow is liberating and empowering and when the perfect outcome arises and the ideal solution is presented, you will know exactly what course of action you need to take and you will do so effortlessly.
This is how life becomes a breeze.
If, on the other hand, you persist with your perpetual planning, strategizing and figuring things out you miss so much of life's natural wisdom, wit and beauty.
And you will probably feel exhausted.
It's stressful when you think you're the only one who can sort out life's problems.
That's where the metaphor of carrying the weight of the world on your shoulders comes from.
It's hard work!
If you want life to feel lighter, do less.
Even just a little less is good.
I do understand that doing less can seem a scary concept.
My human struggles with it.
But my being adores it.

When I do less, and go with the flow, my being starts to vibrate with happiness.
There are always jobs to be done and chores to be completed. But it's the way you approach them that matters.
Sweeping the floor is a job to be done, and if you approach it with your story about never having enough time, working too hard, nobody ever helping you and it's all right for your bloody sister 'cos she can afford a cleaner – you can see how sweeping the floor becomes a really big deal.
Or... you could just sweep the floor
Wow! Who knew housework could be so beautiful?
Even when I have boring admin to do (my human loathes admin even more than housework), I sit down without any agenda and do what I need to do. If it becomes stressful and I feel my story creeping in, I walk away. But more often than not, a perfectly adequate outcome occurs, and I just go with the flow,
Notice I say perfectly adequate, not perfect.
My human is a perfectionist.
My being just is.
This can create tension in my life if I choose to let it.
I choose not to let it.

JUST TAKE THE NEXT STEP.
(MY FAVOURITE MANTRA)

I admit that it's harder to do less if you have a big corporate job and you're expected to be churning out work in order to justify your salary.

Harder, but not impossible.

Remember, it's all in the mind.

If you believe that you have a list of tasks to be completed and deadlines to be met you will feel the stress of all that doing.

Doing less isn't an option.

Doing less will get you fired.

Right?

Not necessarily.

This is not about literally downing tools and refusing to take on more work.

This is about a shift in mindset that takes you out of the story of the human who has an endless To-Do List and not enough hours in the day, and instead puts you into the flow of the Universe where you can be fully present with whatever is occurring and simply take the next step without over-thinking or getting stressed.

Paradoxically, this is a far more efficient and productive way of working. You don't waste endless time and brain space by thinking about all the jobs you have to do, wondering how the hell you're going to squeeze everything in.

You simply take the next step.

No distractions. No stress.

You get into the flow and you let the task be done. That is

when your best ideas bubble up and your greatest work emerges.

This is the essence of less doing, more being.

It is a magic formula that cannot fail.

If you try it and you and it doesn't work, it's only because you are believing that it doesn't work.

You are still trapped in fear, AKA humanness.

Whatever you CHOOSE to BELIEVE becomes your reality.

Stop pretending that you know how the entire Universe works.

Not even Stephen Hawking knew how the Universe works.

Maybe if you miss the deadline and, heaven forbid, you actually do get fired it would be the greatest thing that ever happened to you because it would lead you to a job that you really love and draw you into a different social circle where you interact with people who understand and inspire you and suddenly you feel more content and at peace with yourself than you've ever felt in your whole life.

You cannot know the future. Nobody does.

So embrace the now by being it, not doing it.

Just take the next step. That's all you ever have to do.

QUITTING YOUR ADDICTION TO OVER-THINKING

Stop assuming to know what is best for you.
Quit planning, strategising and thinking ahead – unless it's for practical matters like booking a plane ticket or meeting a friend. That's all fine and is a necessary part of the human existence.
But you do it as and when the moment requires, without your back story, and you don't torment yourself with ruminating on endless permutations of what may or may not go wrong.
That would be psychological torture.
Just book the flight and move on.
Stop analysing and judging.
You don't need your back story to book a flight.
You will only ever drive yourself crazy if you continue to indulge in these very human habits.
Stop caring about how others are analysing and judging you.
This is more torture.
Others will always analyse and judge you. It is inherent in human conditioning and is a side-effect of our mental programming of paranoia. You cannot stop others from judging and analysing you and if your happiness and inner peace depend upon getting top marks from everyone you meet, your existence will be hellish at best.
Bin the need for approval.
The most enigmatic and inspiring people you have ever met in your life are those who walk their own path.

Slow down.
Resist the urge to over-think.
Thinking is a survival tool. It will not induce serenity.
Give more attention to your other senses.
Listen more intently.
Touch and feel with curiosity.
Allow tastes to linger.
Notice how your body feels.
Check in with your breathing.
Explore your field of awareness.
Notice that it extends beyond your physical body.
Where does it end?
Where do you end?
Could it be that you are the entire Universe?
Embrace the mystery and the mystical.
Feel the shimmer of your being.
It is the most beautiful aspect of your existence and the portal to a calm, happy, easy life.

THE BIT WHERE IT ALL FALLS APART

I've woken up to discover there's been an overnight coup. While I was sleeping, my heart has been ousted from its throne, where my mind now sits triumphantly in charge of my entire existence.
To be honest, I felt it creeping in last night.

I put it down to tiredness and expected a good night's sleep to restore my usual serenity.
But although I slept well, I have woken this morning feeling very human and very pissed off.
I cannot see the world today with the powerful clarity that I have come to take for granted.
Ah! Maybe that's it? I've been taking my peace for granted. Not honouring it with as much heart as I should. Not guarding it with enough vigilance.
And in the still of the night, the human crept in and deposed my beloved being.
My human is now firmly in charge.
As I go about my morning I am aware of being stalked by clouds of irritation and depression.
Worse still, my mind has launched a brutal attack, sensing a moment of weakness and grabbing its opportunity to bury my being for once and for all.
It mocks me: "Who are you to write a book about happiness? Ha! What a joke!"
It trawls through the files of my memories and brings forward endless evidence of my failures and incompetence.
Suddenly the future feels terrifying.
I am riddled with self-doubt.
There is such uncertainty.
And I have decisions to make and I don't know what to do.
And I remember that I lived like this for years.
And I remember that life as merely human is hell.

I AM A TOTAL LOSER

I am hopeless.
I am crap.
I am fat.
I should not be writing a book.
Nobody will read the book.
Nobody will like it.
Who do I think I am?
I'm going to look like a fool.
A laughing stock.
Egg on my face.
Idiot.
I'm wasting my time.
I need to get a proper job.
The house is a mess.
There is laundry to do and I'm fannying around with a book.
I am fantasist.
I'm a freak.
A weirdo.
And there is no such thing as the being.
I am human. Just human.
I am wasting my life.

THE F WORD

Instinctively I know my being hasn't deserted me.
How can the heart of what I am ever not be me?
It's just that right now the volume of my mind has drowned out my ability to hear the small, sweet voice of my soul.
When I cannot hear it, it is hard to believe it exists.
And so I use the F word.
Faith.
When my mind rampages and bleakness sets in, I call on my faith.
I know the truth of who I am.
I have experienced the power that emerges when I lean into my truth.
I have evidence of the miracles that occur when I give my life to grace.
The mind has come to taunt me now, to tell me what a fool I am for allowing the being to take charge of my life. It tortures me with images of homelessness, my kids disowning me, the crazy spiritual chick who said that humans have forgotten they are beings. Look at her now, in the gutter. Be warned, people of the world, this is where spiritual folly will lead you.
My mind is vicious and relentless and loud.
I call forth my faith.
I ask it to arise within me to provide a guiding light in this momentary darkness.
And before long, I hear a faint whisper…
Your thoughts are not real.
Your thoughts are not real.
Your thoughts are not real.

AND SUDDENLY I REMEMBER THE TRUTH

And it's like being thrown a rope.
I grab it and begin to climb, one hand over the other as I pull myself out.
I look out my window and see the dazzling sunlight of a glorious autumn day.
The gold and russet leaves aflame with colour.
A pair of blackbirds listening for worms.
A squirrel scampers past.
And I realise I am all of this.
The light frost on the lawn.
The blue tit foraging in the hanging basket.
The patches of lights and shade on the tree trunks created by the sun's low rays.
I continue to climb and the picture becomes ever clearer.
The 'I am' presence within me tingles with a sense of appreciation as I re-affirm my knowing that, without it, I would not be able to witness the divine beauty of this world.
Nor would I be able to see it without my human eyes.
And in a flash I remember why I chose to experience humanity – so that I could taste for myself the sweet and the bitter, the darkness and the light, the highs and the lows.
This being human is a ride, a trip.
It's the Universe having a day out at a theme park riding rollercoasters.

Yes, I am human.
But I am also a being.
I remember this.
And I continue to climb.

I WIN, FOR NOW

My mind senses defeat, for now, and so it slinks away.
I know it will be back.
It only knows the physical and its job is to keep my body alive.
I thank my mind for its dedication and find a job for it to do.
It can remind me about all the human chores I must complete today, renewing a driving licence, posting a birthday card, grocery shopping for the weekend, remembering to collect my son from his dance club later.
My mind is a great PA.
It enjoys the practical day-to-day planning of the human existence.
I know better than to let it take charge of my whole life.
It is too constricted to allow me to experience my wholeness.
But it can only exist because I am a conscious being.
My beingness is the blank screen upon which my life plays out.
No screen, no life.

And so I am back.
I have remembered the truth of who I am.
A little slice of being from the grand universal cake.
A sliver of the Universe.
That's me.
Yippeeeee!

AND IT IS BEYOND GLORIOUS

Suddenly I'm back and life is sweet again.
I'm happy and light-hearted.
The weather seems brighter.
My lover is more loving.
The kids are delightful.
The dogs are adorable.
Humour abounds.
Compassion arises.
Gratitude swells within me.
Other people lose their power to piss me off.
The TV news is less bleak.
The world doesn't scare me.
Synchronicities occur.
Opportunities arise.
Ideas flow.
Words spill onto the page.
It is effortless.

I'm not even trying.
My power feels limitless.
My existence feels infinite.
It is beautiful.
I am beautiful.
My being shimmers with love and grace.
How could I have thought life was a struggle?
How could I have succumbed to the mind and believed its lies?
Everything is clear again.
The truth is obvious.
I am happy and calm.
Life is easy.
So easy.
It just is.

I CHOOSE THIS BEAUTY

And I'm not bitchy.
Or judgey.
I'm not self-critical.
Or self-conscious.
I don't get annoyed about stuff I want but can't have.
I don't get flustered when plans go askew.
I'm not pissed off when people let me down.
It's all so insignificant.

So petty and trivial.
My focus is no longer trained on the detail – the individual stitches of life.
I have stepped back and now I can see the entire tapestry… and it is magnificent!
Even though some stitches may be broken or discoloured, it doesn't matter.
The overall picture is breathtaking.
Perfectly imperfect.
It's so liberating.
I choose this view.
I choose to drop the details.
I know that if I look for fault I will find it.
And if I look for beauty I will find it.
I choose beauty.
I choose to recall my being.
In this moment, I embrace all of me – human and being.
I am no longer ruled by my mind.
I am free.
I know the mind will be back when my guard is down.
It will prowl, waiting in the darkness for a moment of weakness when I get pulled into the story of the human and lose sight of my truth.
I'm not naïve.
I know it will be back.
But right now, I choose beauty.

I REMAIN VIGILANT

What have I learned from my experience?
The mind will never give up.
It will wait for complacency and creep back in to ruthlessly overthrow the being.
It is only doing its job.
Like a self-important bodyguard who wants to run my entire life.
It will fight to reassert its position and authority.
Make no mistake about its ambition.
Remain vigilant.
Watch for signs of an uprising.
Keep it in its place.
You will know when the mind has triumphed because you will feel like crap. The future will seem terrifying and you will be reminded of previous life errors that are evidence of your incompetence.
I spoke to a student yesterday who was experiencing a mind attack.
It reminded her of a blunder she made a decade ago when she accidentally pressed Reply All on a confidential email.
She'd forgotten all about the incident, but her mind hadn't – randomly dredging it up as evidence of her uselessness.
Funny how this happened just as she is deepening her connection with her being.

KEEPING THE MIND BUSY WITH OTHER JOBS

As you deepen your own connection to your being, expect the mind to kick off.
It's not going to go quietly.
It's only doing its job.
It genuinely believes that if you make this existential shift your entire life could fall apart. It will remind you about this frequently.
Don't say I didn't warn you.
Stay strong.
Stay with the heart.
Stay with truth.
Stay with the essence of who you are.
Stay as a being.
Stay as love, peace, happiness and abundance.
And here's some good news for the mind...
Although it lost the top job and is no longer CEO of you, it still has a significant role to play. It can still oversee all the practical decisions of the human – it can manage time, book holidays, pay the bills, make arrangements and do all the essential admin of life. This role is vital and not to be under-valued. The mind will be perfect in this job.
It may not be particularly appeased by this.
Because it still wants to be in charge.
It might think this role sounds boring.
It will want more exciting assignments, like having dreams.

THE BEING IS THE BOSS

The mind can still have dreams, aspirations and ambitions. It can still fantasise about the fast cars, fabulous homes and flashy jewellery. But these are not assets to be acquired at any cost. The mind can come up with great ideas about what would constitute a 'perfect' life. But it cannot be attached to these ideas and believe – as it does now – that they are conditions of happiness.

There are no conditions on happiness.

The being knows this, because the being is happiness.

The being has no problem with gorgeous homes and holidays. In fact, it very much enjoys them. But it does not need them to be happy.

That's the critical difference.

The being is happy no matter what.

The being is love no matter what.

The being is all of these things because it contains the entire Universe in its heart.

The being is who you are.

A radiant, beautiful, abundant being who happens to be here for now in the shape of a human who sometimes feels sad and angry.

It's OK to feel sad and angry sometimes.
It's what all humans feel. Without those feelings of sadness and anger you would not be able to feel the human experience of joy.
You (as a human) would not know light, were it not for darkness.
You would not have any concept of hot, were it not for cold.
You are here as a human to experience the play of inter-related opposites.
It's all part of the game.
Embrace both.
The light and the darkness.
The happy times and the sad.
But do not identify with either.
The sadness you feel as a human is not the truth of who you are.
It is a feeling that has occurred as a consequence of you believing the thoughts of your mind.
Likewise, the happiness you feel as a human is not the truth of who you are.
It is a feeling that has occurred as a consequence of believing the thoughts of your mind.
See all these thoughts come and go as you live out your human experience.
CHOOSE which ones to indulge in.
But do not identify with any.
The human experience is forever in flux.

Watch this from your existence as a being.
And see all thoughts, feelings and moods pass through like clouds in an infinite blue sky.
You have been living your entire life as a human with the mind as your boss.
The mind does a brilliant job at keeping your body alive.
But it is useless at allowing you to feel the effortless state of serenity and joy that flows naturally within your being.
The mind creates thoughts – some happy, some sad.
When you believe the happy ones, you feel happy.
When you believe the sad ones, you feel sad.
What a turbulent existence this is.
You're never quite sure if you're up or down.
One day can feel like hell.
A good night's sleep and suddenly… what was the problem?
This is how unreliable the mind is.
This is how unreliable your sense of stability and peace is when you let your mind rule your life.
There is no basis for lasting peace, contentment and happiness when your mind is in charge of your life.
Nor should there be.
It is not the job of the mind to deliver lasting peace and contentment.
If you want effortless peace and happiness, give more attention to your being.

INTRODUCING THE CHARACTER KNOWN AS YOU

Your human mind has created a very compelling picture of the character known as you.

This character, also known as your ego, lives out the story of your life.

The story really is just a story.

The character known as you really is just a character.

You have a past, a history and memories.

Some of them good, some not so good.

You have a childhood and, chances are, that childhood was not plain sailing.

As a dear friend of mind used to say: "Everyone has their own shit."

Yes, every person does indeed have problems and challenges in their life, as well as a tonne of good stuff that has been blended together into the character known as you.

This character is here in a physical body in this physical world, governed by the physical mind and is doing its very best to survive.

The mind keeps past mistakes alive to prevent you from making them again.

Guilt, regret and judgement are created by the mind. They are not real.

The mind also feeds you a steady stream of dreams and aspirations to drive you to want more, get more and make your future 'safe'. It plays out scenarios of what *might* happen if you do not make the right decisions.

These are projections, created by the mind.
This is fear.
It is not real.
Stop and notice that none of your memories nor your projections are real RIGHT NOW.
Pause your reading for a moment and take this in.
Neither your memories nor your projections are occurring in reality right now.
In other words, right now, none of your memories and projections are real.
They are alive only in your mind.
You keep them alive and hang onto to them to perpetuate this character known as you.
Your character and its story are not real.
They are memory and projection – alive only in the mind.
Right now – they are not real.
The existence that you are experiencing is predominantly thought-based.
Not real.
The existence called being human that you totally identify with is not real.
It is memory, projection and a constructed identity that you carry in your mind.
In your mind.
Your entire life is in your mind.

MORE RESISTANCE

Resistance.
Resistance.
Resistance.
Notice this.
Notice the thoughts that arise from the mind.
Can you see them?
Who sees them?
Who are you?
Who are you really?
Try experiencing life from the perspective of your being.
Stop thinking so much.
Instead, sense and feel.
Give more weight to what you sense and feel.
In today's hard-headed world, this advice may sound flimsy.
Life has become so transactional.
We are all doing business with each other.
We have a personal agenda.
We want the best deal.
We plan and strategise.
We are gunning for the promotion.
Those who sense and feel don't get the promotion.
The top job goes to the best thinker.
Really?
Baaaaaaaa.
Question everything.
Just because it's what everyone believes, doesn't make it true.

Question all the rules.
The human race is self-destructing.
We are not as clever as we think we are.

LESS THINKING, MORE BEING

The brain is a highly sophisticated organ.
It is great at keeping you at the top of the food chain.
It is terrible at making you happy.
Think less.
Sense and feel more.
This is why mindfulness works. It encourages you to be less in your mind, more in your body.
When you walk, you sense the crunch of the leaves beneath your feet.
You hear each footstep.
Every one unique.
A snapshot in time, never to be repeated.
Stay connected to your body and sense the cool air on the back of your hand.
The gentle warmth of the autumn sun on your cheek.
It's very subtle.
Go too fast and you'll miss it.
Stay in your mind and you'll miss it.
Slow down and you will appreciate it.
You will see yourself as part of this beautiful Universe.

You will sense your being.
Your being is the conscious presence that enables your entire perception of life.
I am here.
I am walking.
Leaves are crunching.
The air is cool.
The sun is warm.
Without your body, you would not be able to walk, see, hear and feel.
Without your being, you would have no awareness of your body.

BEING NO BODY

Your body can only exist within the presence of the being.
Your being is what is aware of the body.
In fact, it's not even really a body.
It is a collection of atoms that human minds have collectively labelled 'a body' and you think it's who you are.
Your body is not who you are.
You are nothing.
Nobody.
No body.
You are consciousness currently experiencing life as a person.

A human being.
The human part of you wants to label and categorise everything.
It sees a collection of vibrating atoms in the corner and labels it a chair.
It sits down on the chair and feels comfortable.
The vibrating atoms feel very real.
The body feels very real.
The character known as you feels very real.
In your mind, all is real.
But all of it is thoughts, assimilations, assumptions and projections.
You can enjoy these thoughts.
Enjoy the ride.
But don't identify with any of it.
And if it ever feels like something is missing, that's your calling to check back in with your being and remember the truth of who you are.

VENTURING BEYOND THE PHYSICAL

Thoughts change, vary and fluctuate.
One day I want a new job or I want to lose weight or go on a holiday.
The next day, or maybe later that same day, I've changed my mind.

What is the space within which this changing of my mind can be seen?
Where is the constant within the swirling chaos?
It is the being.
The being is everywhere and it is nowhere.
Nowhere.
Now here.
You are now here.
This is all you have.
This is all you are.
This very moment.
The entire Universe in this very moment.
Everything and nothing,
No thing.
You aren't really the character.
You aren't really any body.
No thing. No body. Now here.
This is the truth of who you are.
Is your mind creating resistance?
Does it hate the thought of being a nobody?
We are all conditioned to aspire to be somebody.
When I grow up I'm going to be SOMEBODY.
And you think that is commendable.
Your mind is inevitably challenging the suggestion that you don't even have a body.
Every time you look in the mirror, you see your body. It is VERY real.
There's all the proof you need this book is nonsense.
Remember that from a quantum physics perspective, what you see in the mirror is nothing more than a collection of

vibrating atoms that your mind interprets as a body.
It tells you that these atoms are more real than anything and that the number one job for the day is to keep this body alive.
And so the story perpetuates... you the character, the body, the life.
Memory, interpretation, assimilation, assumption and beliefs.
Just thoughts.
Whether you CHOOSE to BELIEVE them is entirely up to you.
Your physical form – the body/mind – is just one aspect of your existence as a human being and right now you believe it to be the dominant one.
You believe that you are a human, and that there *might* be something called a soul within you, but you don't really understand the point of the soul and why it's so crucial to your happiness.
Stop giving this to your mind to figure out.
This is beyond the realms of the mind.

LETTING GO OF YOUR STORY (BEST THING EVER!)

Stop asking the mind to help you figure out this so-called puzzle.
The programming of the mind does not have the software required to make sense of this.
Can you see that asking the (physical) mind to explain the (non-physical) heart is ridiculous?
The character known as you is having none of this.
But what if you were to drop that character for a moment?
What if you were to let go of the story of your life – which isn't real anyway.
The great spiritual teacher Mooji calls the process of dropping your story 'The Invitation'.
It is an invitation to experience your true self without the character of your mind, your story, your ego.
An invitation to see yourself as the limitless blank page that you are within the divine book of the Universe.
Let go of all your memories, just for a few moments.
Let go of all your projections, just for a few moments.
Let go of all thoughts about your identity. Your name, your role and your responsibilities in life.
Just for a few moments, ask all these thoughts to leave the room.
Let them all go.
You can get them back later if you want to.
But for now, they've gone.
What's left?

DISCOVERING THE TRUTH

You. Pure you.
You without your story.
You without the programming that says because you've always done it this way you should continue to do it this way.
You without the fears and anxieties that come with trying to predict the future.
Just you.
A pure being.
Sitting here in a human body.
A body with senses that allow you to read this book.
(Note – the senses do not fall away even when you ask the story of your life to leave the room.)
Look how you can function perfectly well without all those memories, projections and that assumed identity.
Look how easy and spontaneous it all is.
Sit with this for a moment and see if you can get a sense of the stillness.
Watch how the mind tries to jump in with assumptions and interpretations.
Simply say – not now thank you – and although the thoughts might be dancing around and trying to get your attention, for now you are refusing to engage.
Notice and acknowledge how you can function perfectly

without your story.
You do not need your story.
You do not need your mind.
What a discovery.

CHOOSING TO BELIEVE

The being (you, without your story) is the part of yourself that you can connect with to experience infinite wellbeing and happiness.
Do not give your happiness to your mind.
It cannot deliver.
It's not in its nature.
Your wellbeing requires your being to be well.
Makes sense?
True, deep, lasting peace and happiness can only be found in the heart of your being.
Learn how to tap into this abundant wellspring of love and your life will change forever.
You will feel whole, centred, peaceful and happy no matter what.
Shitty things might still happen, but you will witness them from this place of extreme serenity and they will not have the power to rock you.
It's up to you now.
How do you want to continue?

Carry on CHOOSING to BELIEVE every thought the mind throws your way?
Experiencing life merely as a human?
Or explore the alternative?
When you CHOOSE to BELIEVE you are only human, you pinch yourself off from guidance and miss all the pointers to your most spectacular and effortless experience of life.

ENJOYING THE BEST OF BOTH WORLDS

A human being is a divine spirit having a physical experience.
Is this true for you?
What are you CHOOSING to BELIEVE?
When your human stays connected to your being, you experience life in pure harmony.
You can enjoy the play of inter-related opposites in the physical world – marvelling at the breadth and depth of experience – but you never lose yourself in any of it.
You are constantly aware of your full existence as a human being – first and foremost a spiritual being, here in physical form.
You carry your sense of universality, love, happiness, faith and grace with you wherever you go.
As you traverse this planet as a human being, as many

enlightened people do, you can truly have the best of both worlds.
You can have a physical body with senses that allow you to experience life. You can have a mind that enables you to make safe, sensible decisions. But sitting above both these functions as the CEO of your entire existence is a being that sees the truth of it all.
It does not get lured by desires, for it already has everything is needs.
It does not get side-tracked by sadness, anger of fear for it knows that in time everything passes.
It does not become obsessed by the temptations of the physical world for it knows that so much is illusory.
It does not go to the mind for happiness for it is eternally abundant with the joy of the entire Universe.

THE TOTAL LIBERATION OF LIVING WITHOUT YOUR STORY

There is such happiness waiting for you.
Such peace. Such bliss. Such ease and grace.
When you live as merely human you pinch yourself off from this great source of love.
And you don't even see yourself doing it.
Even now as you scrutinise these words, you are deferring to the mind.

You keep going to your mind for the answers.
Stop going to your mind for the answers.
Fall effortlessly now into your being and allow yourself to sense what is here.
When non-essential thoughts arise – don't let them pull your focus
If you see them as nonsense, refuse to engage.
If they are more profound, they may have something to teach you.
Experience them, but do not identify with them.
Remember, they are just thoughts.
When memories of the past flare up – stupid things you said and dumb mistakes you made – remain unengaged.
Don't give your power to the mind.
When the practical mind prods you with a shopping list or dental appointment to attend, you can act on that without having to bring your whole life story to the supermarket or dentist's chair.
Experience your life moment by moment with your being as your guiding light.
Don't give your power to the mind.
Have a body but be no body.
Have things but be no thing.
Go places but be nowhere.
Be now here.
It's all there is.
Don't let that pesky mind tell you otherwise.

STARTING AFRESH

Drop your story.
I promise you don't need it.
Start every day fresh. As a human being – a divine spirit having a physical experience.
This is such a beautiful way to live.
Life cannot drag you down.
Instead it is effortless, joyful and powered by immense grace.
All of this is yours for the taking.
Admit where you got it wrong.
Acknowledge that you've been neglecting your being.
It won't care. It will be happy to have you back.
Commit to giving more attention to your being.
Notice how easy it is to re-align your perspective.
A simple shift.
Fuelled by faith.
All you need and all you will ever need is to acknowledge your being.
Do not let your mind tell you otherwise.
Enjoy your life.
It is beautiful.
You are a human being.
Experience the entirety of that, not merely the human aspect.
Honour your being.
Be it.
Embrace it.
Love it.

NO MORE RULES

So let's get practical.
It all sounds great, right?
But how EXACTLY do you go about living wholly?
Living as a human being.
Not merely as a human.
Recognising both aspects of your existence.
The human and the being?
Feeling whole.
Every day.
Every moment.
Here's the great news.
There is no doctrine or dogma required to discover your wholeness.
You don't need any religious beliefs, knowledge or experience.
No ceremonies.
No rituals.
No pledges to make.
Nothing to sign up to.
No church to attend.
No rules to follow.
No commandments to obey.
No cult to join.
No sins to confess.

No self-flagellation – which may come as a disappointment to some.
Nothing to pay.
Nothing to sacrifice.
Nowhere to go.
Nothing to change.
Nothing to fix.
Everything you need is already within you.
It's simply a matter of remembering that your true nature is a human being – a divine spirit here in physical form.
Remember, confirm and reconfirm.
You are a human being.
Experience yourself as both.
See the human. It is physical.
Feel the being. It is spiritual.
You are both.
Embrace your whole self.
This is the key to happiness on this earth.
One tiny lightbulb moment that will illuminate your entire existence.
Eliminate your entire existence?
Kind of.
Let go of the story of who you are.
You mind is hanging on to it, but it's just a story.
A past and a future that are not real right now.
Let it go.
Let it all go.

YOU REALLY DON'T NEED YOUR STORY

The knowledge and experience that you have gained throughout your life will always be there, In the back of the mind, (its rightful place) for you to call on whenever you need it.
Not at the forefront of your mind, dominating every living moment.
Influencing your life.
Suffocating your real existence.
Obscuring your wholeness.
Drop your story now.
See if you can do it.
All memories of the past – drop them for just a few moments.
Refuse to engage.
All projections into the future – seen for what they are.
Illusions.
Refuse to engage.
All ideas about your identity. Outed as a mere story.
Refuse to engage.
Over-ride the mind.
Acknowledge your being.
Sense your non-physical essence.
And see if you can experience the next few minutes of your life like this.
Like a human being.
Try it. Try just a few seconds of being.

(PAUSE)

Is that it?
Notice that the mind wants more.
More instruction.
More tips, tricks and techniques.
More yoga, breathing and meditation.
Surely there has to be more?
The mind always wants more.
But there isn't any more.
It really is this simple.
Drop your story and choose to experience each human moment as the being you truly are.
You are a human being.
First and foremost a being, in human form.
You are not your story, your thoughts, concepts and ideas.
Notice that the space of the being is vast.
It cannot be contained.
It cannot be threatened.
Nothing non-physical can be threatened.
A being cannot be threatened.
You cannot be threatened.
You are a being.
Feel it.
Confirm it.
Enjoy your human experience and the play of inter-related opposites.
But do not lose sight of who you truly are.
A being.
Eternally safe.

Wanting for nothing.
Nothing.

NO STORY. NO DRAMA. NO EGO.

When the mind jumps back in, watch it.
You can see that you are not your mind.
Stay as the watcher.
Watch the mind do its job.
Its job is to keep your body alive.
It will generate a stream of thoughts that are ultimately fear-based and designed to keep your body alive.
You are not your body.
You are not your mind.
You see them both.
You – the being.
A pure, universal being.
Sense again now your universality.
It is irrefutable.
The mind will try to refute it.
But thoughts are not real.
They are not who you are.
When you notice the mind taking over with a story, call yourself out on it!
Refuse to indulge in the nonsense.
Begin to see how much of what you give your energy to is illusory.

It's BS.
See how the human loves the BS, the story, the drama.
The being does not get involved.
It is neither interested, disappointed nor amused.
It just is.
You will soon begin to see where the human is addicted to drama.
The mind loves to gossip and judge.
The being has no interest.
Stay detached.
Observe but don't engage.
This is not cold, it is beautiful.
Although your mind will try to tell you otherwise.
The mind no longer has dominion over you.
It is a practical tool to be used throughout the human experience.
But it is only one aspect of the human experience.
Don't let it call the shots.

ESTABLISHING YOURSELF IN THE INFINITE

Infinite happiness lies within the heart of your being.
Why pinch yourself off from this?
If you genuinely want to feel happiness as a human being – the solution is very simple:
Acknowledge yourself as a being.

You don’t know how to do this?
You are like a beautiful big chocolate trifle saying: “Errr… can someone please show me how to be a chocolate trifle.”
You already are everything that you aspire to be.
Open your eyes.
Feel your truth.
Stop giving all your power to the mind.
The mind can’t make you happy.
You don’t even need to find happiness because you already ARE happiness.
The mind will tell you otherwise.
But you can ignore its commentary.
When it comes to practical matters, consult the mind and take its advice.
When it comes to happiness, do not consult the mind.
The mind might make you smile and laugh sometimes, but it cannot deliver the profound peace and lasting contentment that you crave.
You are about to end this book.
Your mind can’t wait.
Ignore it.
You are a human being.
Humans suffer.
Beings don’t.
Be your being.
Drop your story.
Do it again now.
No past, no future, no identity.
Feel your heart centre.
Sense your being.

Just be.
Deal with each new moment as it spontaneously arises.
There will be challenges.
That's fine.
Witness them as the being that you are.
Don't fuel their existence with your story.
Challenges will pass.
Your humanness will ultimately pass.
You being will remain forever.

ENJOYING THE RIDE

Enjoy your time as human by acknowledging yourself as a being.
It's so liberating.
And quite the ride.
You get the best of both worlds because you can experience the physical – the highs and the lows, the bitter and the sweet, the darkness and the light.
But none of it effects the truth of who you are.
A being.
An expression of the Universe, here today in human form.
You are naturally peaceful, happy, supported, and free.
Of course you are.
You just are.

The simple truth of how to feel happy is to remember that you are a human being.
That's it now.
Done.
Stop going to your mind for happiness.
You won't find it there.
You will find it in the heart of your being.
Because happiness IS the heart of your being.
Feel, acknowledge, confirm and reconfirm.

FOLLOWING YOUR HEART

I don't have all the answers.
I'm not pretending to have all the answers.
I know very little.
My human likes to think it's really smart.
My being knows that truth.
My human didn't write this book.
My being did.
My human never knows what's going to happen.
I had no intentions to write a book today.
I was planning to go to the shops.
But I wrote a book.
I don't know how it happened.
If I had listened to my human it wouldn't have happened, and you would not be reading this.

But I honoured my being, who had something to say.
I used my human hands to type the words.
The perfect functioning of human and being.
Because I am a human being.
And now it is done.
My human thinks it's ridiculous.
My human says don't publish. It's embarrassing. You're wasting your time.
My being says do it, do it, DO IT!!!

CHOOSING HAPPINESS

So I did it for you.
I published because I listened to my being.
And now you are reading it because you listened to your being.
Your being is constantly guiding you towards a happy, calm, easy life.
There is no question of that.
I cannot even begin to tell you how beautiful life is when you practice the art of being, because honestly… it is beyond words.
All I can say is that you do not have to go searching or seeking.
Everything you need is already within you, waiting patiently to be acknowledged and appreciated it.

Whatever you appreciate, appreciates.

And so when you give your being the value it deserves, it will bring tremendous value to your life, and you will know beyond all doubt that you are supported and held and loved.

Your being is beyond the story of the human known as you.

Refrain from giving the human so much attention and choose to give more to the being.

Every time you bat away a thought or a feeling that arises from the human, you liberate your being a little more.

Choose to engage less with your human.

Choose to engage more with your being.

It is raining now. My human hates rain. My being accepts what is. I have a choice.

I choose to engage with my being.

It is raining.

And that's just how it is.

Such peace.

And out of peace arises contentment.

And out of contentment arises happiness.

And out of happiness arises bliss.

And suddenly life is calm, happy and stunningly simple.

FINAL WORDS

Every human is searching for happiness.
Being is happiness.
Every human will find happiness when it finds being.
You will find happiness when you find being.
Nothing you can buy or experience from an external perspective will substitute the bliss of being.
When you put the mind in charge of your happiness it will take you in the wrong direction.
Put your being in charge of your happiness.
Start today.
Right now.
And look what happens. You discover that you are already everything you were looking for.
What a discovery!
Finally, you can call off the search.
You can live the remainder of your life as a human being knowing that there is a dimension to your existence that can never be threatened nor has anything to be afraid of.
And so you can relax.
Your being is the essence of who you are. It is what makes your presence on this very planet possible. It is the Universe within you.
Allow this aspect of yourself to guide you and life will be simple and effortless.
It will be powered by grace.
In harmony with all that is.
Get out of the way of yourself.
Listen to your heart and simply take the next step.
This is the lost art of being.

PART TWO

QUESTIONS & ANSWERS

Over the following pages you'll find a handful of questions that commonly arise when I am talking with students who have enrolled in my classes and workshops about the art of being. Some of these questions might have come up for you as you were reading through Part One. My hope is that you will find your answers over the next few pages. If you don't, feel free to email your question to me:

jacqui@jacquimacdonald.com

Q. How am I supposed to slow down when my life is hectic? It feels like every second of the day I have to be somewhere, doing something. I literally cannot do less. My life would fall apart.

Your life would not fall apart. This is a story that your mind created and you are blindly believing. Question everything. Perhaps some aspects of your life would fall away, but how do you know that wouldn't be a good thing? You are holding onto your busyness because it is part of your identity. Being busy is valued in our society and often we wear it like a badge. We collectively champion the woman who can do everything – excel in a high-flying career whilst also being the perfect mum. But we do so at our own peril.

Being busy is not a crime, but nor should it be an aspiration.

The truth is you don't have to be as busy as you are. You can always choose to do less. You will soon discover that the less you do, the more space you create to let life flow naturally. Suddenly you realise that you don't need so much forward planning and organisation. You deal with whatever requires your attention moment by moment. This frees up a lot of brain space and energy.

So how do you begin? How do you make that initial shift?

It is all in your mind. Right now you believe that you have to do it all in order to make life work. You have no faith in the Universe to support you. None. Zero. No wonder life feels like a struggle.

Look around you for proof that the Universe is pretty good at doings its job. The sun rises every day. The earth keeps on turning. Seasons come and go. It has all the big stuff covered, and yet you don't trust it with your life. You think you can do a better job. And that is actually quite funny.

When you carry the belief that you have to do it all to stop your world from falling apart, you disrespect the Universe. And as long as you continue to carry such belief, it will linger as your reality.

The first step is to find your faith. Without faith you stay in the struggle. Once you have faith you feel more comfortable letting go of some of the responsibilities and tasks that right now you feel are essential. You drop a few balls from your impressive but insane juggling act and guess what... Life doesn't fall apart. It gets easier. So you drop a few more and suddenly life gets sweeter and sweeter. And although you're no longer a contender for Best Juggler of the Year, you don't care. Because you feel great. You have more time to spend with loved ones and do stuff that makes you feel like you. And you have more space to listen to the wisdom and guidance that is leading you to your effortlessly happy life. And so the story continues.

Find faith and the rest will follow.

Q. So I'm supposed to accept what is. Does that mean I have to give up on all my dreams and ambitions and just roll over and be grateful for whatever crumbs life throws at me?

I love this question because it is so typically human! Notice how fearful it is. Classically paranoid and the perfect example of the programming of the human mind. Remember, the purpose of the brain is to keep your body alive and it does not want you to have any whiff of your universality and immortality. It is telling you that acceptance of what is will leave you without what you need to be happy and safe.

So here we are again. Notice that you have a CHOICE here of what to BELIEVE.

Believe your mind and stay stuck on the wheel of

suffering, trapped into the programmes of paranoia and desire.

Or take a leap of faith.

Trust that the Universe always has your very best interests at heart and knows way more than you do about what will make you happy. When you CHOOSE to BELIEVE this truth instead of what the mind is offering, you fall into a glorious stream of abundance and grace and everything you need to be happy will be provided.

It may be that you need a lot less to be happy than you currently think, and so choosing to go with the being rather than the human could be the perfect path for you to encounter a life that is calm, happy and effortless.

Break free from the slavery of your mind. It is not allowing you to even experiment with the vast opportunities that might be waiting for you should you shift your perspective.

Your mind is not the boss. You are.

Q. I like pretty things. I have a fabulous collection of shoes and handbags that I love. I enjoy flying first class and staying in great hotels. Do I need to give all of this up to feel inner peace?

Not at all. If the Universe has provided you with the means to have luxury, why not enjoy it? The secret is to make sure you don't identify with this luxury or imagine that it represents who you are. Don't demand or expect luxury wherever you go, feeling annoyed if you don't get what you are accustomed to. That's very human behaviour, and it will lure you back into the lair of the mind quicker than you can say Jimmy Choo.

If you notice yourself becoming irked because standards are not meeting your expectations, see if you can step backwards and observe the mind running a movie-reel. Can you find evidence of a story that suggests material wealth and fancy experiences make people happy? This is a BS story. It's up to you if you CHOOSE to BELIEVE it.

If you do get caught up in this story, your ego will inflate as your sense of self-entitlement escalates. This is when you find yourself on a slippery slope.

It can be more challenging for wealthy people to feel happy because they are keen to identify with and take credit for their success. You can see how that's a harder story to let go of than one that's beset by poverty and disappointment.

Whatever the narrative is, rich or poor, you have to let it go.

Neither your Jimmy Choos, nor the human strutting around in them, are who you really are.

If the human has to sell her shoe collection on Ebay due to a sudden cash-flow crisis, she will likely feel loss, almost like part of her identity has been auctioned off. "I loved those shoes. They were so me."

Get real and wake up. You are a being. You do not need

sparkly stilettos to feel divine. Recognise this and you will feel equally happy with or without your luxuries.

In the meantime, why not enjoy them?

Q. When you say forget your past, isn't this promoting the practice of denial?

Connecting with your being, AKA you without your story, is not the same as being in denial. It's simply a matter at looking at things from a new perspective and recognising the truth of the present moment.

When emotions arise for the human, the being will help you deal with them because those who are in touch with their being are empowered with an incredible sense of discernment. When feelings surface, the being can see from its neutral perspective whether they are genuine and need to be experienced and allowed. Or whether they are just the human regurgitating an old story and getting caught up in the drama.

There is a powerful difference between processing and wallowing, and knowing your full self as the human *and* the being will enable you to differentiate.

I was at a party recently and got chatting to a woman called Kath who told me her mother had left her as a child, leaving her father to raise her. She was pouring in the wine as she poured out her sorrows, explaining how life had been so difficult. I asked if she minded me enquiring how old she was and she told me she was 56. 'So this happened to you almost 50 years ago and it is still really hurts.', I said to her as gently as I could.

"It's a major part of who I am," She explained. "It defined me."

"If you choose to believe that, then of course it will be true for you."

There was a flicker in her eyes, but her mind was not willing to give up so easily.

"What am I supposed to do?" She said. "I can't change the past."

"No, but you can be less attached to it and the idea that it is a cornerstone of your identity. You can't change the past, but you can change the present and the future. Keeping this hurt alive is not serving you. It's not making you happy. It is programming the future to be just like the past. Can you let go of the story about the girl whose mother abandoned her. It still happened. But it's not happening right now. Who's here right now? How does *this* moment feel, without your story?"

She paused for a second, taking everything in. "Wow," she said. "I never thought of it like that."

Q. Isn't that the same as telling Kath to deny her feelings and the experience of her mum leaving?

Quite the opposite. It is encouraging her to see the truth of what is real right now.

If she were genuinely feeling emotions of grief and loneliness, observing these feelings from the place of the being would allow her to experience those live emotions in the moment, without the story making it feel heavier.

The being is like a laser. It has the power to cut through the story and get straight to the truth.

Witnessing and experiencing your human emotions from the perspective of the being delivers unprecedented clarity for you to explore and negotiate your emotions in the moment. You will quickly discover that your own personal hard-luck story has less bite, less attack. Separate the feelings from the story and remove the drama. Deal with what arises, as and when it arises.

Be clear about what actually happened to you and how it made you feel. Don't look at past wounds through the lens of conditioning. We are all brought up to believe that life should be a certain way and that it is desperately sad if something goes wrong.

Question everything.

When you are in touch with your being you have a more vivid sense of the vast and infinite grace of the Universe, and so rather than wallow about past pain, you can fully experience your human emotions and look for the wider wonder and wisdom to emerge.

You may even discover a blessing in something you previously assumed was a curse.

Q. Shouldn't we be talking about our past hurts. I thought maintaining good mental health meant talking about our emotions and being honest about old wounds.

It's true that the human body can hang on to emotion and energy relating to pain from the past. Mental scars, if you like. As humans, talking about these emotional wounds can help heal them by allowing the energy to come to the surface and move away. But you have to be willing to let them move away.

Sometimes we subconsciously hang on to the pain because it has become such a big part of our identity. We are scared to let it go because we feel like we will be losing a part of ourselves.

This is a very human perspective which arises because the programming of the human mind is fear-based. The mind clings to past hurts as evidence that the world is not safe and that you could die at any moment. This keeps you trapped in the mode of paranoia and desire, pulling you back onto the wheel of suffering and spinning it ever faster so it's almost impossible to jump off.

When you can view your wounds from the perspective of the being, who wants for nothing because it already has the entire Universe in its heart, you naturally let the pain go.

When you sense that you already are all that is, you have nothing to lose, and you understand with profound clarity that letting go of pain does not mean you will be diminished in any way.

It is impossible to diminish the being.

Q. You don't understand. I suffered a real trauma in my past and you're saying I should just let that go? Act like it never happened? I can't do that.

Nobody is suggesting that you act like the past never happened or blot it out of your mind. What you suffered was real at the time and of course it has affected the person who you are today. But take notice of that phraseology. It has affected the person.

On a human level you suffered trauma and the mental and possibly physical scars are still with you. But you are not merely human. You are also a being. Where you choose to place your attention will define your reality accordingly.

There is a significant part of you that sees what happened and accepts it purely for what it was.

As hard as your human experience was at that time, it may have opened up an opportunity for great soul growth and certainly it has brought you to where you are right now – learning about the greatest discovery in the human kingdom so that you can live the remainder of your life with a profound sense of peace.

We cannot pretend to understand or know how the Universe works, but our beings inherently know that it is loving and supportive and always has our best interests at heart.

The human is quick to label experiences either good or bad. The being trusts that life is unfolding as it should. It refrains from judgement and maintains its vibration of peace.

If you hang onto the pain of past trauma, you stay stuck as a human. Letting go is often a beautiful opportunity for you notice that you can forgive and accept. And in doing so you will be released from your human cocoon to realise that you have the wings of a butterfly.

Q. I want to let the pain go but it keeps coming back.

You are a human being. Part human, part being.

You are going to feel human pain and emotion. Otherwise you would not be human.

You do not have to try to be purely being.

You can observe your human experience from the perspective of the being.

This gives you space and clarity.

Often when the human is under stress, or tired, or hungry or unwell, emotions will feel more pronounced. Notice this and, as the being, and cut your human some slack.

Do not deny your human emotions. Feel them within your wholeness as a human being.

Allow the full spectrum of your feelings to be however they need to be.

But do not be attached to any of them.

Be smart enough to know the difference between processing and wallowing.

Talk about what happened, get help if you need it.

Expose the pain.

Refrain from embellishing it with a story.

A story will fuel the pain.

Accepting and embracing the purity of the pain will engender divine healing for the human, powered by love and support from the Universe.

Q. Is there a ritual or an exercise I can do to let go of my pain?

Yes, and it's a ritual you can perform in every moment of your life. You have more power than you think to programme your life to be as you would like it to be. The first step is realising this.

When your thoughts stay stuck in the past and when they get pulled into the uncertainties of the future, you are letting your mind rule you and staying stuck as human.

When you notice yourself judging, complaining, defending yourself or making excuse – you are staying trapped in your human cocoon.

Practice mindfulness to become more aware of the thoughts when they creep in and see what they have to teach you. Every time you notice a human, fear-based thought arise, replace it with a love-based feeling and you will have chalked up another tiny triumph for the being. Keep on doing this and your healing will naturally progress.

There will come a time when you see past pain for what it is.

If it has helped you emerge from your cocoon, you may even become grateful for it.

In the meantime, be gentle with yourself. Slow down. Feed yourself well. Acknowledge your humanity while honouring your divinity. Let go by not giving the story so much attention and the rest will unfold by itself.

Stay present. Notice what is real right now and what is being created by your mind.

Q. If I feel a strong emotion rising, what should I do?

A useful technique that I use when I get pulled into the drama of human emotions is called the RAIN contemplation. RAIN is an acronym for Recognise, Allow,

Investigate and Non-Identity. Here's how you go through the process.

When you feel a powerful negative emotion arising and it's so strong that it's obscuring your sense of being, press pause on whatever you're doing and take a moment to experience RAIN.

Step 1. Recognise. Begin by recognising and labelling the emotion. 'This is fear.' 'This is worry.' 'This is grief'... Or whatever it is you might be feeling. See if you can label the emotion, to the best of your ability.

Step 2. Allow. For a few moments, or as long as it takes, allow all the emotions to be exactly as they need to be. Notice the thoughts swirling in your mind. Notice the physiological impact on the body. The racing heart, tightened tummy or shallow breath. Give everything permission to be exactly as it needs to be and fully experience your feelings. You might even be brave enough to invite more powerful emotions in. "Come on mind, throw your best punch!" Remember that bullies retreat in the face of strength.

Step 3. Investigate. After feeling the full force of your emotions, move on to exploring their context. E.g. *Of course, I'm feeling angry. I've just been dumped by someone I trusted.* Or... *It's natural to be sad, my Granny just died.* See if you can also investigate who exactly is experiencing the emotion. Consider this: If you can see the emotion – you cannot be the emotion. The part of you that is able to recognise and label the emotion is different from the one gripped by it. Try to give all your attention to the one who watches. This is your being. It will witness the human grappling with the emotion from a place of peace and neutrality. Your being is like the sky – infinitely clear blue. Clouds may come, seeming to obscure the sky. But they can never affect the true nature of the sky. No matter what, the sky is always clear blue.

Step 4. Non-Identity. Confirm now that human emotions are real and painful, but they are not the truth of who you are. They will come and go like clouds in the sky. For now, let it rain while you stay as the sky.

Q. I'm confused. You encouraged me to send away all thoughts and memories about the past so I could experience my being. But you also said to feel emotions as they arise, even if they pertain to the past. Which is it?

As you go about your daily life, experiment with getting into the habit of living each moment without your story. When you wake in the morning, try spending a few minutes dropping your story and connecting in to your being. As your day unfolds, notice the spontaneity, beauty and challenges that occur for the human and see if you can maintain your broader perspective as a being.

Remember your thoughts are not real and you don't have to get hooked into the story of each and every one of them. Stay neutral. Stay as the being. And witness the most magnificent unfolding of your own life.

If a powerful emotion does arise for the human, grief for

a lost loved one or fury at an injustice, give that emotion time and space to express itself within the human. Experiment with the RAIN contemplation, and when you are ready, return to experiencing your life without your story.

Q. So are you basically saying we should live in the moment?

Sort of. But it's more than that. When you live in the moment as a human you run the risk of being pushed and pulled in all directions and life can feel very turbulent. If you live every moment believing the stories of the mind, you are on shaky ground.

But if you can drop your human story and experience the natural unfolding of life from the perspective of the being, you see that everything is just as it is.

Living in the moment as a human is different from living in the moment as a human being.

My human doesn't like chilly weather. When I have to go outside in winter my human gets grouchy and I find myself wishing it could be different. My being teaches me to embrace what is, so as I move around with cold toes and a strong desire to be indoors and warm, I don't get so drawn into the story of 'hating the cold' that would make me feel really pissed off if I let it.

Try both and see which feels better for you.

If my human had its way, life would be sunny and sugar coated every day. Although too much sugar can become sickening, can't it? When life is comfortable, there is no desire to explore our true existence.

When life is challenging, it often forces us to ask serious questions about our purpose here on this planet. These questions can lead to a dramatic spiritual awakening that will reveal the greatest experience known to mankind – the full realisation of yourself as a human being.

In my own experience, if I took all the happiest, most thrilling moments of my life and bundled them into one, it would not come close to the profound joy and sense of peace I feel when I'm fully in the flow of my human AND my being.

Each moment is an opportunity to embrace the being and experience this captivating bliss.

Q. I've read that in order to fully actualise as human being, you have to study with a master for years. Is this true.

If you believe it to be true, it will be true for you.

Q. But surely I need to have a dedicated meditation practice and spend a lot of time in silence in order to experience my being.

It's true that you need to slow down and get out of your head. But in my experience, everyone has the ability to sense their being, because it is the ultimate truth of who they are.

I've worked with students who do little or no meditation and yet are able to drop their story and allow their being to emerge almost instantaneously.

If you think it's going to be hard work, it will be.

But that would be a story.

It's up to you what stories you CHOOSE to BELIEVE.

Whatever you choose to believe will become your reality.

Q. So all my years of yoga and meditation are wasted?

Not at all.

Nothing in life is wasted. Not even the bad stuff. They were all essential steps on the path that has finally brought you here. Be thankful for all aspects of your past as a human. Even the really challenging times had something to teach you. In fact, it is the challenging times that have the most to teach you.

Nothing in your past is a mistake if you learned from it. Be grateful for your entire human experience in this lifetime and the fact that you are being given clear guidance that now is your time to wake up and rediscover the lost art of being.

Meditation, mindfulness and yoga are wonderful ways of slowing down and getting in touch with your body. They reduce the volume of the mind making it easier for you to hear the voice of your being. Practices like these are a great way of creating space for the being to emerge. But you could practice meditation for years and never connect with your being. Likewise, you could realise your wholeness without ever placing one toe on a yoga mat.

If you do yoga, meditation or mindfulness, try dropping all expectations from your practice. So no goals, projections, outcomes or desires. Just show up and be empty. Then simply take the next step.

Q. I've tried and tried but I can't get it. I can't get a sense of my being. Please help me.

Stop trying so hard. It is only your mind telling you that you cannot get it.

How can you not be what you already are?

Your story is obscuring the truth.

Next time you are lying in bed, sitting on a bus or soaking in the bath – experiment with dropping your story.

Make a pact with yourself that for the next five minutes you are not going to engage with any thoughts relating to your past, your future or your identity.

The thoughts may still be there skulking around in the mind, but you have agreed not to engage with them.

If the mind needs something to focus on, try repeating the word: 'Empty'.

So you're on the bus or in the bath and your senses are still working... The water feels warm, or the person next to you is fidgety and annoying. But you remain empty, empty, empty.

Drop all your attention to your heart centre and continue to feel and sense from there.

Don't go to your mind.

How do you feel without your story?

Can you get a sense of your being? Of the field of awareness in which your entire experience of life unfolds.

Notice this field and explore it.

Does it have any physical shape, form or boundaries?

Stay with the field of awareness for as long as you can, resting your attention here in the space of the being.

Notice how spontaneous and easy life is when you don't drag your story around with you.

Experiment with experiencing the rest of the day, or as much of it as you can, without your story.

For further guidance, there are hundreds of videos by Mooji on YouTube that will point you to the truth of your being. If there is a calling in your heart for this, you will be guided to the ultimate discovery.

You don't have to worry about a thing.

Q. I can sense my being but I get pulled back into the identity of the human so easily!

Slow down. Be gentle with yourself. And practice switching your focus back to the being as often as you can. It will come. Unless you tell yourself that it won't.

Q. I've heard that awakening can be quite dramatic. Uncontrollable laughter or tears or both. Or shaking and convulsing. Will this happen to me?

It might, it might not.

Have no expectations. Stay empty. Drop your story of awakening even. The more of a story you have, the more your being will be obscured. Drop everything. And allow what is naturally there to emerge.

The more of yourself you can let go of, the more of your self will be revealed.

Q. But how will I know if I've done it?

There may not be any great fireworks, but you will know because life will start to feel lighter. Dramas that troubled you in the past will appear trivial and you will wonder why you ever felt upset. You will start to see the human with all its strengths and weakness, but you will stay detached from it all.

My human can be smug, arrogant and impatient. I witness this from the perspective of the being. My being is not disappointed or angry at the human. My human is after all, a human, and pride is part of its makeup. My being does not try to change the human. My being just is. And as my day unfolds, sometimes with my human behaving immaculately, other times being a real dick, my being observes it all from its space of neutrality and enjoys the vastness and spaciousness of simply being.

There is space within my being's Universe for the full spectrum of human emotion.

It all comes, and it all goes.

I observe everything and identify with nothing.

When I lapse and give power to my mind, I feel weakened.

I feel lonely, desperate and depressed.

When I remain as my true self I am untouchable.

Q. You've shared a lot. But could you just give me some really practical advice so I can process and begin to practice specifics?

That's such a human request! But it's a valid one. In theory, you don't need to do anything other than remember the truth of who you are to start living from your natural place. But the likelihood is that you are so strongly identified with the story of the human that you'll have to be proactive in cultivating the awareness of your being. This may take some effort at first, but in time it gets easier as your faith builds up and the dominance of the human disintegrates proportionally.

Over the next few pages you will find a collection of pointers and experiments that I use and share with my students to help them reprise the art of being. Some are really straight-forward, others a little more out there. Try the ones that appeal to you and remember to keep an open mind.

If you notice strong aversion to any particular exercise, that's a sure sign of resistance from the mind. It is kicking off which suggests it senses danger. If it were me, I would pour my heart into that particular exercise as I bet it will be the most powerful.

The whole purpose of the book and the following guidance is to get you into an elevated perspective of giving less importance to your humanness, and more importance to your beingness. So be wise to thoughts that try to pull you back down into your habitual way of human thinking.

Once you've got to the end of the book, try reading it

again (it's only little) with your heart not your head and see if you can sense a softer perspective emerging. Allow the words time to sink in and drop any and all expectations.

Expectations are the currency of the mind, but they hold no value for the being.

PART THREE

HOW TO REPRISE THE LOST ART OF BEING.

Lifestyle Guide

I know you're really busy and the last thing you need is more stuff on your To Do List. The good news is you don't have to 'do' anything. But you do have to 'be' in a way that is different from how you've been living until now.

Over the next few pages you will find ten of my favourite learnings, experiments and activities that I weave into my every day life to allow my being the space it needs to emerge.

Every day is different. I don't have a disciplined and time-bound practice that I religiously follow. I just listen to my heart about what I need, and the Universe gives me guidance.

Some days I feel totally out of sorts and I know I need to spend an hour with Mooji or sit quietly or go for a walk in the woods.

Other days I am so naturally alive with being that it requires no effort at all.

Remember that what you appreciate, appreciates.

So I totally embrace these good days as the gifts from the Universe that they are and sure enough… they are becoming more frequent. The stressy human days are diminishing respectively.

Give this stuff a whirl as and when your heart tells you to.

Some of it will require an element of effort at first because you aren't used to 'being' this way. You are in the habit of the human. Breaking any habit requires an element of focus and discipline, but not for long.

Honour what you discover and it will naturally bloom within you.

Be vigilant about the voice of the mind. It will try to pull you off the peace wagon. Every now and then it will succeed. Don't give such tumblings any more significance than what they are. Get yourself back on that beautiful, blissful wagon as soon as you can.

Here's how you begin…

1. SLOW ALL YOUR HORSES RIGHT DOWN

Your human is so caught up in the doing and the busyness of life that it leaves little or no room for the being to be experienced.

You have more choice about the pace of life than you admit.

There is stuff you could say no to.

It's a matter of shifting your priorities.

You race through your To Do list feeling a sense of accomplishment as you tick off each line item, but the satisfaction is fleeting and before long the list is as long as ever.

Where in your day do you allocate time to just be?

How often do you pause to do nothing, to give your

body the space it needs for restoration and rejuvenation?

Often when we live at a brutal pace our bodies will eventually step in and force the issue.

This happened to me. I suffered adrenal exhaustion thanks to a twenty-year corporate career where proving myself and climbing the ladder were my primary goals.

Enforced rest enabled more space and time to just be. And the rest is history.

I was lucky it was just my adrenals I fried. Other beings' bodies have not been so lenient. Strokes, heart attacks and mental breakdowns have become commonplace. Not to mention the C word. Don't wait for a physical crisis to force yourself to rest.

Slow down, starting now.

If you haven't done a Mindfulness Course yet, get signed up. There are teachers in almost every town so get onto Google and find one near you that looks fun and friendly.

If attending classes isn't for you, read a book or find online resources. The internet is full of them .

Mindfulness will teach you to become more aware of what is going in your own brain. Rather than automatically assuming you must live at pace and be your best self every day, a good mindfulness teacher will help you see that this is merely a story that can be dropped in a heartbeat.

Mindfulness will also teach you how to be more present in your body, engaging with all your senses, consequently giving less airtime to your mind.

The less importance you give to the mind, the less significant your human woes will seem.

Slowing down is the essential first step in reconnecting with your being.

Slow down is not just a catch phrase, it's should be taken both literally and practically.

Slow everything down: The way you eat, drink, think, talk and walk. Slow down your conversations with your loved ones. Slow down the time you give to yourself. Enjoy long luxurious baths instead of rushing through a shower. Slow down your morning routine and your evening rituals. Slow it all down and begin to get a sense of a greater awareness than your current rushing perspective is offering. Slow down and take in the depth of your moment-by-moment experience. Keep a journal to write (slowly) about what you are noticing. Slow down enough to see that your thoughts are not inevitable and that you have more power over them than you realise.

Slow down.

Pause.

Breathe.

Slow down.

2. NOURISH YOUR BEING WITH CALM-INDUCING FOODS

I can feel the nervous energy racing through my veins.

The thumping in my heart.

The tightness in my tummy.

Why oh why did I have Nutella on toast for breakfast?

I should know better.

I'm well aware that sugar ignites my central nervous system, activating my fight/flight response.

My mind becomes fuelled by the adrenaline and cortisol rushing through my veins.

It takes control of my operating system, asserting its authority and declaring my being a silly myth.

And all hell breaks loose. Again.

It's harder to hush my mind when I have stimulated my central nervous system.

I know this.

Caffeine, alcohol, sugar – even my favourite dark chocolate.

All these substances are stimulants and boy do they stimulate my mind.

I am a calmer, happier, more peaceful human being without them.

Being human – I continue to take my chances.

A nibble here, a sip there.

Sometimes I get away with in.

This emboldens me to taste a little more.

It inevitably ends the same way – a jittery body, a crowing mind and a loss of connection to my being.

I'm not saying you have to be a teetotal, sugar-free vegan to find inner peace.

I'm simply equipping you with information that you can experiment with yourself.

Indeed, don't take my word for it.

Don't take my word for any of this.

Intellectual understanding is useful but it is nothing without direct experience.

Try for yourself a day with less sugar, less carbs, less caffeine and less alcohol.

See if you feel less stressed.

The less wired your body is, the quieter your mind will be.

I promise.

It is hard to hear the whisper of the being if you are in the middle of a full-on rave.

I've yet to come across book about spirituality or mindfulness that talks about the importance of diet. For me, and my students, what we eat is fundamental and it's the first thing I address with my rookies. Become more aware of the foods that inflate your human (alcohol, sugar, carbs, caffeine) and educate yourself about foods that infuse the physical body with a sense of calm.

And take supplements that support a heathy central nervous system. I cannot be without muti-vits, Magnesium and Rhodiola to support my battered adrenals.

A calm body helps hush my rampaging mind, allowing my being the space it needs to be felt.

Peace sets in, and my quiet, happy life unfolds accordingly.

Being hungry or tired will also make you feel more human. Hunger and tiredness are threats to your physical survival (if you are tired you are less aware of threats and less able to fight them off). Your fight/flight mode will go into overdrive flooding the brain with all the stress hormones that makes it powerful. It is hard to overthrow the mind when it has been fortified and empowered.

Do what you can to eat well and sleep well.

Physical calm engenders spiritual bliss.

3. FIRE YOUR MIND AS CEO OF YOU

This is the big one.

Confronting a bully can be daunting. But once you've done it you can enjoy a new sense of freedom that will change your life forever.

Your mind does not want you to connect with your being because it doesn't want to lose control. It will do whatever it can to keep you trapped so it can retain its position as the boss of you.

As I have said before, it is only doing its job.

But you are in charge of the mind. It is not in charge of you.

So grow a bigger pair of balls or boobies up and start calling the shots.

All your life you have paid ultimate respect to

your mind and the guidance it gives you. You are now empowered.

You do not have to let it dominate you.

Remember, you can CHOOSE which thoughts to BELIEVE.

You always have the power to choose.

The practical mind is very useful and makes a great Personal Assistant… making short-term plans and taking care of your life admin.

The psychological mind is the one to be wary of.

It doesn't mean to cause torment.

Actually, it doesn't care. It has no interest whether you are happy or not. It only cares about keeping you alive.

When thoughts arise that are particularly troublesome and drag you back into the human realm, write them down so you can eyeball them in black and white.

Ask yourself. *"Is this thought true? Is it factually accurate and undeniable true?"*

For example, thoughts like: *I'm such a loser. I'm so unlucky in love. I'm crap at my job. I'll never be able to achieve my dreams. Life is hard. There is no way to escape my struggles.*

Question all these thoughts and scrutinise them from your perspective as the being. You will soon out the lies and stop the mind in its bullying tracks.

Instead of habitually going to the mind for answers to a problem, drop your awareness into your heart centre and see if you can find a different response.

Ensure you give yourself enough time to do this exploration and know that if you do it while wired on wine, sugar or insomnia – you will likely only hear the voice of the mind.

Again, a good mindfulness course will help you realise that you are not your thoughts and that you have more power over your mind than you think.

Spending a small amount of time and money on re-calibrating your thought system will be the best investment you ever make.

You cannot have a calm, happy, easy life if you continue being a slave to your mind.

Do whatever it takes to find your freedom.

And know that the entire Universe is rooting for you and willing you on! Be the hero of your own movie. Have your own real-life Shawshank Redemption or Truman Show moment and be the one who breaks free.

You don't have to live this way anymore.

4. DROP YOUR STORY – YOU REALLY DON'T NEED IT!

You reprise the lost art of being quite spontaneously when you release the story of your human.

Simple.

But not always easy.

If you are anything like the billions of other humans on this planet you will be very much attached to your story and your identity as a human. Your story is the entire narrative of who you are, stemming from as far back as you can remember, right up to this precise point in time.

In fact, your own story may even begin before you were born. Significant tales that you were told about parents, grandparents and even ancestors can have an influence on your current character, personality, beliefs and thought patterns. AKA your story.

For example, a young African American woman who learns that her grandparents were subjected to the violence and brutality of slavery may understandably carry a sense of defensiveness and injustice, even if she never met those particular relatives.

We also have the conditioning of our times to add to our story. I was one of millions of women brought up to believe we could 'have it all'; meaning family, career, social life, the works. This myth destroyed the health of many a good woman in recent years, myself included. The story of failure crept in for those of us who weren't quite Superwoman. It blighted our every move.

Stories of upbringing, childhood, school days, teenage years, first loves, broken hearts, broken friendships and broken dreams shape the way we think, believe and act today.

No matter what happened to you in the past, it counts as story. Even moments that were powerfully devastating only exist right now as memory – a story kept alive by your mind.

This endless collection of events of your life, some big some tiny, are all filed together in your mind under I for Identity. Collectively they make up your story, which is ultimately who you believe yourself to be.

The more you cling to that story and use it to influence and justify your thoughts, actions and reactions – the more entrenched in your human you remain.

When you let go of your story, you willingly relinquish all reference points about how life should be. You don't wipe your brain completely, forgetting how to ride a bicycle or what side of the road to drive on. All practical information you need stays in the practical mind to be called upon as and when required.

What you drop is the story of the psychological mind. You approach each moment with fresh eyes, free from the conditioning of your particular past. This makes your existence joyful, light and spontaneous. You are not bound by thoughts of what life should be like for 'you'. You are open to the mysteries, the twists and turns of fate that the human mind cannot even begin to fathom.

On the days when I'm able to let go of my story I find life fascinating and fun. Even when shitty stuff arises – a surprise bill or a run in with somebody rude – I'm able to experience whatever is happening without bringing all my past regrets, fears or annoyances to the situation. Nor do I make projections – i.e. predictions of future scenarios based on my experiences of the past.

I am simply fresh, spontaneous and open to what is.

I am being, and I am letting life flow.

I talked you through the exercise of dropping the story several times earlier the book, but, let me again offer this brief guidance that I use, inspired by Mooji's Invitation.

Make a pact with yourself that for the next five minutes, you will not engage with any thoughts that arise relating to your past. Likewise, add to the pact a promise that you will not engage with any thought relating to your future. Finally, promise to yourself that you will not engage with any thoughts relating to your identity – including your responsibilities, family scenario, health status or employment. Either ask these thoughts to momentarily leave the room, or practice allowing them to drain out through an imaginary hole in the soles of your feet.

You can do this. It's easier than you might think.

It shouldn't take long to complete the exercise. Five minutes or so. When you are done – notice what or who remains. It's you without your story. Pure you.

Get to know this you. It's your being. And it will bring you more happiness than you can imagine.

5. CONNECT WITH NATURE TO RECALL THE WONDER

When I was having a wobble while writing this book – the bit where my brain took over and made me feel like shit – you'll notice that pausing to appreciate nature played a big part in getting me back on track. It works every time.

There is something about taking time to acknowledge the wonder in living creatures such as birds, wildlife and trees, that reminds us of the wonder within ourselves.

Likewise, you may find it easier to connect with your

own being when you spend slowed-down, quality time with beings other than the human variety. Humans will inevitably reinforce your humanness. Unless of course you are fortunate enough to know humans who embody and honour their beings, in which case hang out with them as often as you can!

If, as is more likely, your circle of friends does not include a handful of enlightened masters, then carving out time to be with beings other than humans will do you the power of good. Spending time with animals can remove your ego, unless you are trying to assert your authority over them. The simple act of sitting with a dog, cat or other furry being and either petting, playing or observing will ignite a natural peace within you.

Even better for inspiring a sense of your inner divinity is spending time with tree beings. I am a huge lover of the Japanese art of Shinrin Yoku – or forest bathing as we call it here. I adore trees and deliberately moved house recently so I could live on the edge of the forest, meaning I get daily inspiration from the magnificent spiritual tree beings that are wondrous metaphors for the divine within us all.

The unfathomable power of the Universe that is encoded within a tiny acorn to enable its growth into a mighty oak tree is the same unfathomable power within you. The developing oak tree doesn't worry about its pace of its growth, or whether it is taller and more majestic than its tree neighbour. It just allows its own growth to unfold in time, according to the will of the Universe.

The oak tree neither struggles nor toils. And yet it is mighty. There is much we can learn from this.

We overlook the fact that without trees our human survival would be impossible. Trees take in the carbon dioxide we breathe out and convert it into the oxygen that gives us life. This is a miraculous process and a tangible reminder that we are connected to the Universe. We are all part of one great eco-system.

There is a wealth of evidence to prove (to the cynical human) that a walk in the woods is good for our health. Scientific research has shown that it reduces cortisol in the body and therefore alleviates stress. It has also proven to assist healing of major health conditions.

I believe this is because trees subconsciously spark a memory within us and the lost art of being is re-ignited. With a deeper sense of the divine, the human being comes back into balance and natural order is restored.

Right… I'm off to hug a tree.

6. EXPLORE YOUR FIELD OF AWARENESS

This is one of my favourite games and is a powerful tool for shattering the myth of the human. You can practice it anywhere… On the train, walking the dog, in a business meeting… I like to do it last thing at night as I'm falling asleep. It sends me off to the most delicious slumber. Here's how you do it:

Begin by noticing that your awareness is not

constricted to within the four walls of your mind, or even the limits of your body.

Notice that you can hear sounds far away and see objects into the distance.

In other words, your field of awareness stretches as far as your senses can perceive.

Look out of a window and notice that you are aware of everything that you can see, hear and feel.

This vista of your observation is your field of awareness.

Explore the quality of what you previously assumed was just empty space.

Get really still to enjoy this experience and let yourself feel from your heart centre as you begin to notice that what makes up your experience goes far beyond your body and mind.

This is your field of awareness and it is where your being resides.

Become enthralled by this field and notice whether it stretches even further.

Very often you have a sense of what is beyond the eyes and ears, even when you cannot physically see or hear it. You cannot always see the sky and yet you always know it's there. You sense it. Close your eyes and notice what it feels like to sense that the sky is there.

Even if you are sitting in an enclosed room you are somehow aware of the space beyond.

This is so cool.

Play with becoming more familiar with your personal field of awareness and noticing where, if anywhere, it ends.

Exploring your field of awareness can be an intriguing

and even exhilarating experiment and before long you realise… *holy shit, I am actually the entire Universe!*

Yep, it's true.

You are in fact the entire Universe.

Your body and mind are just one tiny expression of that Universe, manifesting as a person so you can experience, for a short time, what it feels like to be physical.

Look at all the stuff you get to experience and feel as a human. What a trip! But do not identify as only this little mind and body or you constrict your experience and pinch yourself off from your full power.

Stay vast.

It is infinitely more fun to stay vast.

Don't think about this with your mind. Your mind will only produce a mental construct here and that by its very nature is limited.

Explore your being with your being. It is thrilling!

What is the essence of your own personal field of awareness.

Is it infused with stillness and peace? Is there a resounding sense of knowing about it? Can you feel the forcefield of love?

My heart simply soars when I tune into my vastness and I feel it vibrating and buzzing with the divine electricity of life.

I choose to keep my attention here.

7. STAY TUNED IN TO YOUR BEING

Remember that in every moment you have a choice. You can choose to give all your attention to the human, believing that you are the story that the mind is perpetuating.

Or you can stay vast and infinite, making the human stuff seem trivial.

When your kids are acting up, the human is likely to feel rattled. You might end up shouting and getting stressed as you find yourself wishing your kids could be different and wondering what you did wrong to deserve such wilful offspring.

When stressful situations arise and you give all your attention to the human it will engorge itself with frustration, regret and projections. It might even bring up memories from your own childhood, sparking feelings of self-pity, sadness and guilt (it loves a story!) At this point, you might reach for a glass of wine.

But there is another choice.

Ignore the mind and see if you can drop all stories. For example, let go of all conditioning and expectations about how kids 'should' behave. Drop all thoughts about your own childhood. Don't even go there when the mind is luring you with projections of how your kids will end up if you don't nip this cheeky behaviour in the bud. Step back and notice, from the perspective of the being, that it is what it is: Teenagers being stroppy.

If you feel like you want to ignore them and walk away, do so.

If you feel like you want to ask them, from a measured and loving place, to stop being such little shits, do so.

Either way, remain unaffected. Don't get caught up in the drama and the story.

It is what it is.

You can apply this process to any situation.

Even when there is no situation, get into the habit of dropping the story and stay tuned into your being. Choose not to engage with past, present or sense of identity – and progress with each moment accordingly.

Stay with your being and the sense of neutrality and spontaneity. Stay empty. It is more blissful than you might imagine.

When you get a glimpse of your being, acknowledge and appreciate what you have experienced. You are in a minority, and what you are discovering is not only life changing, it is potentially world changing.

Every time a human being wakes up to the truth of who they are, another sliver of global peace is restored.

Every time you choose to respond from your being rather than react from your human, you contribute to an overall energy of love which touches not only those in your immediate circle but also the entire planet. Your contribution is more powerful than you realise.

Honour your being by taking time every day to re-establish your connection with it. Spend a few minutes first thing in the morning to remember the truth of who you are by consciously letting go of the constructed character in your mind. It can take less than sixty seconds. When you get really good, it can take less than one.

Make time throughout your day to check back in notice where your attention is falling. If the mind has the reins and the story of the human is driving the experience, shift your perception to realign with the more universal aspect of yourself and see what happens when you allow life to unfold, rather than directing it.

Be extremely vigilant and know that the mind will take any hint of an opportunity to topple your peace.

Practice gratitude. Enjoy your tranquillity.

Remember that in every single moment you can CHOOSE what to BELIEVE.

Reclaim your power.

Regain your consciousness.

Reconnect with harmony.

Return to love.

This is the lost art of being.

8. OBSERVE WITHOUT INTERPRETING

This can be another fun, trippy exercise if you allow it to be. You might find it hard at first, but it won't take long before you get the hang of it. If it feels like a chore, let go and get on with your day. Trying too hard is always counter-productive. It should feel more like an intriguing experiment than a piece of homework.

The purpose of this exercise is to break the habit of

letting the mind put labels on everything it experiences. This automated practice of interpreting and allocating an assumed meaning to all that you perceive will keep you trapped in a very physical experience. You perpetuate an established value to whatever you encounter, never pausing to question whether it is real or true for you personally.

When you are able to press pause on the mind's habitual tendency to analyse, interpret and label, you free up a broader perspective and enter the realm of the being.

Here's how it's done.

As you go about your day, notice everything.

You will be accustomed to operating on autopilot, which is the mind's favourite gear because it makes you more efficient. It stops you from being distracted by stuff the mind feels is already comprehended and boxed off, therefore requiring no further enquiry.

This is helpful if you are entering the World Multi-Tasking Championships.

But it means you miss a lot of the magic that resides in the seemingly mundane.

So, when you consciously switch off your autopilot and allow your senses to fully engage, you upgrade your ability to notice… and suddenly life becomes more colourful.

Notice not only the trees but the myriad of different shapes, shades and textures that appear within them. The bark, the leaves, the roots, the branches and the birds.

Notice the busyness of other people as they rush around their day – most of the time on autopilot.

Notice clothing, hairstyles, complexions, expressions and even other people's energy.

And here's the challenging bit.

See if you can observe all of that without making any judgement, analysis or assumption whatsoever.

Try your absolute best to not apply any meaning at all.

This is where the fun begins.

You begin to see news headlines, angry drivers, grey clouds, annoying text messages, unwashed dishes and rude people as...well, nothing more than what they are. Rather than leap into your story and bring layers of interpretation to all of these potentially irritating or anger inducing events, you just see them for what they are, and you move on.

You can be a little less rigid when you experience the good stuff because blue skies, happy faces, funny text messages and waggy-tailed dogs have all been sent to make your being tingle.

But nonetheless, resist the urge to identify with even them. Just see them for what they are and allow any warm glow to contribute to an overall feeling of happiness, and an appreciation of the emergence of more grace and joy in your life.

Soon you will develop a kind of detachment from what you currently perceive as reality.

Detachment?

Aha. Notice whether your mind jumped in here assumed detachment might render you cold and aloof, unable to relate to others or empathise with their feelings.

This is not true.

Detachment empowers you with a magnificent sense of discernment and enables you to get your own story out of the way when encountering the plight of another. If a friend comes to you in tears, you are able to fully be there, listening with your whole being without your human getting pulled into the story of her human's drama.

The practice of observing without interpreting, and ultimately detaching, is a rich training ground for the art of being. You will soon start to get a sense of how different it feels to experience life as merely physical versus your true nature as a vast spiritual being currently having a human experience.

Enjoy this life changing shift in perspective.

9. YOUTUBE YOUR WAY TO ENLIGHTENMENT

I have shared with you the quirky stuff I often do to embody the art of being. Each experience contributes to a beautiful and consistent connection with the Universe, infusing my life with a natural sense of joy and ease.

Here's my big confession. The practice that has contributed most powerfully to the development of my own consciousness has been… err… watching TV.

Yep. I have to admit it. Telly has played a huge role in my enlightenment.

But not just any telly. In fact, my appetite for watching mainstream TV shows has dwindled significantly. I find them hard to tolerate and unless it's something I'm really interested in, TV for the most part, is a turn off.

But boy do I love YouTube.

Once upon a time you would have had to travel to India and beyond to hear the teachings of great spiritual masters. Nowadays you just flop on the sofa and start surfing. It's brilliant!

My favourite pastime is to switch on the box and invite the greatest living sages, wise women, gurus and mystics into my very own living room where I can devour their every word while sipping tea from my Buddha mug. I don't even have to get dressed.

There are so many profound and authentic teachers out there. They each have their own unique slant on what we've been discussing in this book, but much of it points to the same thing. The most influential that I have encountered include Eckhart Tolle, Marianne Williamson, Byron Katie, Rupert Spira and, my favourite, Mooji. They vary in terms of their 'weirdness'.

Marianne's teachings, based on *A Course in Miracles*, are very practical and straight-talking which for some cynical humans makes her a more relatable teacher.

I also like the mystical stuff.

Eckhart Tolle is a little more esoteric as he explores the power of now with his own brand of humility and humour. He is a truly enlightened being and his talks hold so much truth.

Byron Katie also uses humour (in a big way!) to help people see how ridiculous their stories are. Her workshops often end in people laughing hysterically as they realise they have been carrying around a totally fake identity. She's brilliant!

Rupert Spira is more serious. He is eloquent and logical as he enquires into existence and exposes the truth.

And my beloved Mooji is like God personified. His heart is full of insights and knowledge bequeathed by a line of genuine spiritual masters. He has the kindest eyes, the warmest manner and a sparkling, mischievous wit that you wouldn't necessarily expect from a sage. I could watch his videos for hours (and I do!). Infinite wisdom delivered with unending patience. I always experience a shift in consciousness when I sit down with Mooji, and he is my go-to guru when I'm feeling my most human and need to be reminded of the truth.

I spend about an hour a day watching Mooji and, in truth, his YouTube videos have become the backbone of my spiritual practice.

I don't do this out of discipline. I do it because for me there is no better way to spend any free time than immersing myself in the words of a master and deepening my bliss.

An hour per day is by no means a prescription. Do what feels right for you. Or do nothing at all. Your intuition will guide you accordingly and you may well find other teachers that resonate with you more than the ones I have mentioned.

Either way, listening to the wisdom of these remarkable beings will help you over-ride the mind and get back to the truth of who you are.

Explore, experiment and enjoy... ideally in your pyjamas.

10. AND FINALLY... STOP TRYING SO HARD

The feeling I get when I'm fully in touch with my being is the most thrilling yet serene experience in the world. Words cannot even describe how wonderful it is to feel like I am alive with and powered by grace, and that I do not have to worry about outcomes or strategies in order to be my best self.

The only drawback is that the blissed-out feeling is kind of addictive.

Once you've tasted it, you want it all the time.

If you're not careful, you fall into the seekers trap and you become so intent on trying to get back into the flow that you take yourself out of it entirely.

This is a schoolboy error that I think every seeker experiences at one time or other.

And it isn't fun.

You get little glimpses of grace then it feels like it gets snatched away, leaving you feeling desolate and often incredibly lonely.

The irony is the harder you try to re-establish your connection, the further you push yourself away.

This is because your efforts only serve to affirm the idea in your mind that you are first and foremost human.

Can you see the trap?

So, the secret to all of this is the very same secret to life: Stop trying so hard.

Do less to be more.

Tune into the vast and infinite wisdom and allow it to flow through you.

When you feel yourself becoming frustrated, take your foot off the gas and just chill. Don't even think about the human or the being. Just go for walk or make some tea or read a lovely novel that has nothing to do with the Universe.

Without effort you will notice the fresh air or the pattern on the tea cup or the beautifully crafted sentence and there it is… your being is back. In truth, it never went away.

You can never not be what you fundamentally are. But if you try too hard you fall straight back into doing mode and the being becomes obscured.

Slow down. Eat well. Drop your story and then just let it all happen.

It cannot not happen.

It already is.

Whether you CHOOSE to BELIEVE this is entirely up to you.